Joe Stahlkuppe

Giant Schnauzers

Everything About Purchase, Care, Nutrition, Training, and Wellness

Filled with Full-color Photographs

Illustrations by Michele Earle-Bridges

CONTENTS

GIANT SCHNAUZERS: AN INTRODUCTION

The large, black dog heard an unusual sound, a sound that was out of keeping with the normal nighttime noises of its home. Instantly alert, the big dog left its bed and went in search of the source of the sound. While silently padding along the carpeted floor, this canine guard was the end result of a century of careful breeding for strong guard and family companion dogs.

This dog was just another in a long line of Giant Schnauzers bred and trained for working and for protecting their humans and their homes. The rough-coated, bristle-browed dog was not very different from its distant ancestors. These ancestors patrolled Bavarian farms and factories at the turn of the twentieth century, served valiantly in the world wars, provided canine backup to police and security guards, and loved and were loved by countless humans of all ages.

After finding a sleepy child returning in the dark from getting a drink of water, the Giant Schnauzer used its furry muzzle to guide the drowsy youngster gently back to bed. After feeling assured that no danger threatened, the dog went back to its bed until the next time a first-class guard dog might be needed. Such is the work of the typical Giant Schnauzer.

The attributes that made the Giant Schnauzer an ideal working dog translate well to making him an excellent family companion and protector.

"Schnauzer, oh you've got a Schnauzer?" The first breed that comes to mind when *Schnauzer* is mentioned is probably the immensely popular Miniature Schnauzer. This perky breed, called the *Zwergschnauzer* in Germany, ranges in height from 12 to 14 inches (30 to 36 cm) tall. The Miniature Schnauzer is consistently in the top 20 in most popular dog breeds and is usually the number one ranked terrier in the American Kennel Club (AKC).

Another Schnauzer breed is available—the sturdy, medium-sized *Mittelschnauzer,* or Standard Schnauzer. It can stand from 17.5 to 19.5 inches (44 to 50 cm) tall. Although greater in size but fewer in numbers than the Miniature Schnauzer, the Standard Schnauzer is not usually ranked even in the top 100 most popular breeds. The Standard Schnauzer is the original of the three Schnauzer breeds and is listed by the AKC as a working breed.

The AKC working-dog group is made up of nonherding, nonhunting breeds as diverse as the Alaskan Malamute and the Great Dane. Joining the Standard Schnauzer in this group is the impressive and powerful Giant Schnauzer, which ranges from 23.5 to 27.5 inches (60 to 70 cm) tall.

Bred for specific work by purposeful dog breeders, the Giant Schnauzer (commonly referred to as simply a Giant) is the product of years of breeding for definite goals to produce a versatile, capable, and hardy working dog. That the dog breeders achieved these goals and also produced a beautiful, eye-catching dog breed is a definite plus for the Giant Schnauzer. The Giant is more popular than the Standard Schnauzer and much less popular than the Miniature Schnauzer, usually ranking just within the top 100 breeds based on numbers of dogs registered each year.

Part of a Varied Family of German Breeds

While the Giant is the largest of the three, separate Schnauzer breeds, it is but one of several well-known, working-dog breeds that were developed in Germany. The Great Dane, the German Shepherd, the Rottweiler, the Doberman, and the Boxer have all achieved greater fame than the Giant Schnauzer, yet the Giant is still quite popular in Europe. Even with the notable security dog reputations of some other German breeds, the Giant Schnauzer maintains a strong following in this area within its home country.

Kin and Near Kin

The Schnauzers have long been linked with another group of German breeds, even to the sharing of common ancestry. The original Schnauzer was once part of a close genetic alliance with the versatile German Pinschers.

Eventually, the need arose for a medium-sized farm dog to do all manner of canine work. The desire to have a rough-coated Pinscher for these tasks is thought to

The Giant Schnauzer is one of several large, working-dog breeds that have become very popular around the world. From the left are the Great Dane, the Doberman, the Giant Schnauzer, the Boxer, and the Rottweiler. The popular German Shepherd Dog is a member of the herding family of breeds.

Black (in a shorter working trim) and pepper-and-salt (in show condition) are the only colors allowed in the Giant Schnauzer standard, with the blacks being more commonly seen.

have resulted in the development of the original Schnauzer. At one time, the Schnauzers and the Pinschers were considered merely variations within the same breed.

The German Pinschers were smooth-coated. Adding a rough-coated variety would give the breed greater usefulness in the harsh German winters and in various cattle-driving and vermin-killing roles. Crosses were therefore made to produce a wire-haired Pinscher. Sometimes litters would have both smooth and rough puppies. The smooth puppies were referred to as Pinschers while the pups with furry *schnauzes* (German for "muzzle") were called Schnauzers.

History of the Giant Schnauzer

From the middle of the last millennium onward, German cattle farmers around Munich worked their cattle with large drover dogs. These nondescript dogs were good workers, but they were a varied lot. In an effort to bring genetic continuity to the larger cattle dogs, the popular medium-sized Schnauzer seems to have been used as both a visual and working model and certainly as a genetic contributor.

The ragtag group of existing local cattle dogs were most probably crossed with Standard Schnauzers of the day. Some authorities insist that the black Great Dane also played a part in adding height and substance to the Giant. Other authorities point to the Belgian cattle dog, the Bouvier des Flandres, as a very likely ancestor of the Giant Schnauzer.

The results of this canine cocktail were then carefully bred to resemble a larger and more powerful version of the well-accepted Standard Schnauzer, even in the same solid black or pepper-and-salt colors. These larger dogs were called *Munchener*s or Munich Schnauzers and later Giant Schnauzers. The big dogs were produced with all of the working ability, protectiveness, and versatility of the original Schnauzer but in a larger package. Interestingly, the larger size (and the bigger appetites) gradually caused the German cattle farmers to lose interest in this king-sized Schnauzer.

The saga of the Giant might have ended there in gradual extinction. However, these big Schnauzers had attracted somewhat of a following in Munich and in surrounding towns as large watchdogs. They became brewery and butcher shop guards and thus survived to be more and

Many authorities believe that the Bouvier des Flandres is in the background of the Giant Schnauzer. Both breeds are very similar in appearance and temperament.

Below left: Giant Schnauzers have long been prized for their power, beauty, and good companion dog attributes.

Below right: The Giant Schnauzer's size, strength, and trainability suited it to a variety of necessary functions in Germany after cattle droving was discontinued.

The Giant is one of the most stately and beautiful of the working breeds.

Below left: Grooming is essential for maintaining the dog's appearance and health and also serves to bond owner and dog.

Below right: A Giant Schnauzer is often the ideal choice for an owner who can assume and maintain the "Alpha" position in the relationship.

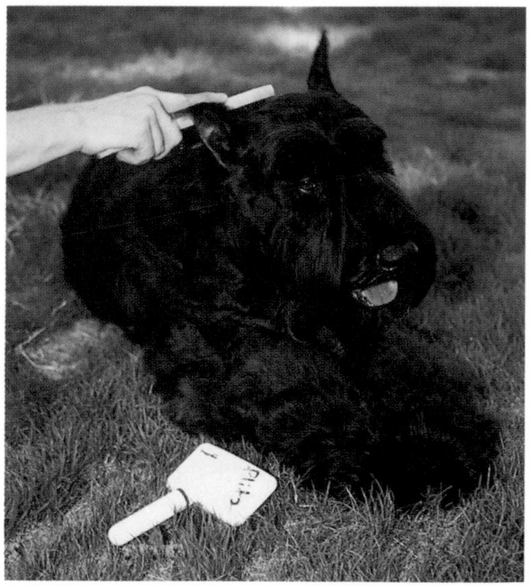

more unified into a breed. By 1900, this largest Schnauzer, now commonly called a Giant Schnauzer, was an attractive and impressive breed that gained an immediate base of admirers when it was introduced in Munich dog shows.

During both world wars, the Giant Schnauzer took on new duties and became a respected and battle-tested war dog. The Giant also gained a following as an excellent police dog. Without making this transition to other needed work, the Giant might have, for the second time in its young life, faced extinction.

When the Second World War ended, the Giant Schnauzer saw an expansion of its role as a law enforcement dog. Because it is very intelligent, hardy, large enough to be a definite deterrent, and extremely trainable, the Giant became one of the most sought after dogs in Europe for these purposes. The former cattle drover that became a butcher and beer hall dog, then war dog, also became an accepted family protector.

Physical Appearance

The Giant Schnauzer is a giant among Schnauzers but not among dogs in general. The true canine giants are breeds like the Saint Bernard, the Great Dane, the Mastiff, and the Irish Wolfhound. The Giant Schnauzer is about the height of the Doberman with less weight than the average Rottweiler. The breed has greater size and a more powerful appearance than its former prototype, the Standard Schnauzer.

As opposed to the Standard and Miniature Schnauzers, there seem to be more black Giants than ones with the pepper-and-salt coloration. The vision of a large black dog coming out of the night to protect its home and family has made the Giant a popular choice as a home guardian breed. Because it is strongly territorial and innately suspicious of strangers, the Giant makes an excellent watchdog that doubles as a good, but quite large, family pet.

Temperamentally, the Giant is a potentially aggressive dog. Such a dog needs just the right owner to gain control and keep control of an energetic and very bright canine. This fortunate combination of beauty, power, brains, and grit have made the Giant Schnauzer, in the hands of the right persons, one of the most versatile of all breeds.

American Kennel Club Standard

General description: The Giant Schnauzer should resemble, as nearly as possible, in general appearance, a larger and more powerful version of the Standard Schnauzer, on the whole a bold and valiant figure of a dog. Robust, strongly built, nearly square in proportion of body length to height at withers, active, sturdy, and well muscled. Temperament which combines spirit and alertness with intelligence and reliability. Composed, watchful, courageous, easily trained, deeply loyal to family, playful, amiable in repose, and a commanding figure when aroused. The sound, reliable temperament, rugged build, and dense weather-resistant wiry coat make for one of the most useful, powerful, and enduring working breeds.

Head: Strong, rectangular in appearance, and elongated; narrowing slightly from the ears to the eyes, and again from the eyes to the tip of the nose. The total length of the head is about

The three Schnauzers vary greatly in size. In terms of breed history, the medium-sized Standard Schnauzer is the oldest of these breeds, with the Giant and the Miniature coming along much later.

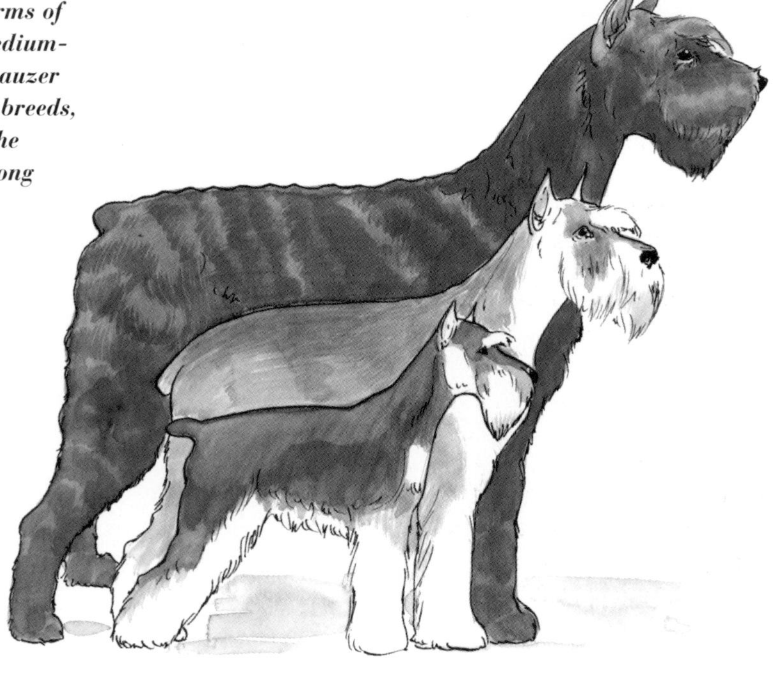

one-half of the length of the back (withers to set-on of tail). The head matches the sex and substance of the dog. The topline of the muzzle is parallel to the topline of the skull; there is a slight stop which is accentuated by the eyebrows. *Skull*—(occiput to stop). Moderately broad between the ears: occiput not too prominent. Top of skull flat; skin unwrinkled. *Cheeks*—Flat, but with well-developed chewing muscles; there is no "cheekiness" to disturb the rectangular head appearance (with beard). *Muzzle*—Strong and well filled under the eyes; both parallel and equal in length to the topskull; ending in a moderately blunt wedge. The nose is large, black, and full. The lips are tight, and not overlapping, black in color. *Bite*—A full complement of sound, white teeth (6/6 incisors, 2/2 canines, 8/8 premolars, 4/6 molars) with a scissors bite. The upper and lower jaws are powerful and well formed. *Disqualifying faults*—Overshot or undershot. *Ears*—When cropped, identical in shape and length with pointed tips. They are in balance with the head and are not exaggerated in length. They are set high on the skull and are carried perpendicularly at the inner edges with as little bell as possible along the other edges. When uncropped, the ears are V-shaped button ears of medium length and thickness, set high and carried rather high and close to the head. *Eyes*—Medium size, dark brown, and deep-set. They are oval in appearance and keen in expression with lids fitting tightly. Vision is not

The Giant Schnauzer standard describes the breed very clearly and will answer the questions of experienced owners and novices alike.

In today's world, ear cropping is only a matter of fashion honoring tradition. The Giant Schnauzer standard does not require cropping and even describes the ideal appearance and carriage of natural ears.

impaired nor eyes hidden by too long eyebrows. *Neck*—Strong and well arched, of moderate length, blending cleanly into the shoulders, and with skin fitting tightly at the throat; in harmony with the dog's weight and build.

Body: Compact, substantial, short-coupled and strong, with great power and agility. The height at the highest point of the withers equals the body length from breastpoint to point of rump. The loin is well developed, as short as possible for compact build.

Forequarters: The forequarters have flat, somewhat sloping shoulders and high withers. Forelegs are straight and vertical when viewed from all sides with strong pasterns and good bone. They are separated by a fairly deep brisket which precludes a pinched front. The elbows are set close to the body and point directly backwards. *Chest*—Medium in width, ribs well sprung but with no tendency toward a barrel chest; oval in cross section; deep through the brisket. The breastbone is plainly discernible, with strong forechest; the brisket descends at least to the elbows, and ascends gradually toward the rear with the belly moderately drawn up. The ribs spread gradually from the first rib so as to allow space for the elbows to move close to the body. *Shoulders*—The sloping shoulder blades (scapulae) are strongly muscled, yet flat. They are well laid back so that from the side the rounded upper ends are in a nearly vertical line above the elbows. They slope well forward to the point where they join the upper arm (humerus) forming as nearly as possible a right angle. Such an angulation permits the maximum forward extension of the forelegs without binding or effort. Both shoulder blades and upper arm are long, permitting depth of chest at brisket.

Back: Short, straight, strong and firm.

Tail: The tail is set moderately high and carried high in excitement. It should be docked to the second or not more than the third joint (approximately one and one-half to three inches long at maturity).

Hindquarters: The hindquarters are strongly muscled, in balance with forequarters; upper thighs are slanting and well bent at the stifles, with the second thighs (tibiae) approximately parallel to an extension of the upper neckline. The legs from the hock joint to the feet are short, perpendicular to the ground while the dog is standing naturally, and from the rear parallel to each other. The hindquarters do not appear overbuilt or higher than the shoulders. Croup full and slightly rounded. *Feet*—Well-arched, compact and catlike, turning neither in nor out, with thick tough pads and dark nails. *Dewclaws*—Dewclaws, if any, on hind legs should be removed; on the forelegs may be removed.

Gait: The trot is the gait at which movement is judged. Free, balanced and vigorous, with good reach in the forequarters and good driving power in the hindquarters. Rear legs and front legs are thrown neither in nor out. When moving at a fast trot, a properly built dog will single-track. Back remains strong, firm, and flat.

Coat: Hard, wiry, very dense; composed of a soft undercoat and a harsh outer coat which, when seen against the grain, stands slightly up off the back, lying neither smooth nor flat. Coarse hair on top of head; harsh beard and eyebrows, the Schnauzer hallmark.

Color: Solid black or pepper and salt. *Black*—A truly pure black. A small white spot on the breast is permitted; any other markings are *disqualifying faults. Pepper and salt*—Outer coat of a combination of banded hairs (white with black and black with white) and some black and white hairs, appearing gray from a short distance. *Ideally;* an intensely pigmented medium gray shade with "peppering" evenly distributed throughout the coat, and a gray undercoat. *Acceptable*—All shades of pepper and salt from dark iron-gray to silver-gray. Every shade of coat has a dark facial mask to emphasize the expression; the color of the mask harmonizes with the shade of the body coat. Eyebrows, whiskers, cheeks, throat, chest, legs, and under tail are lighter in color, but include "peppering." Markings are disqualifying faults.

Height: The height at the withers of the male is 25½ to 27½ inches, and of the female, 23½ to 25½ inches, with the mediums being desired. Size alone should never take precedence over type, balance, soundness, and temperament. It should be noted that too small dogs generally lack the power and too large dogs, the agility and maneuverability, desired in the working dog.

Faults

The foregoing description is that of the ideal Giant Schnauzer. Any deviation from the above described dog must be penalized to the extent of the deviation.

The judge shall dismiss from the ring any shy or vicious Giant Schnauzer.

Shyness: *A dog shall be judged fundamentally shy if, refusing to stand for examination, it repeatedly shrinks away from the judge; if it fears unduly any approach from the rear; if it shies to a marked degree at sudden and unusual noises.*

Viciousness: *A dog that attacks or attempts to attack either the judge or its handler, is definitely vicious. An aggressive or belligerent attitude toward other dogs shall not be deemed viciousness.*

Disqualifications

Overshot or undershot.

Markings other than specified.

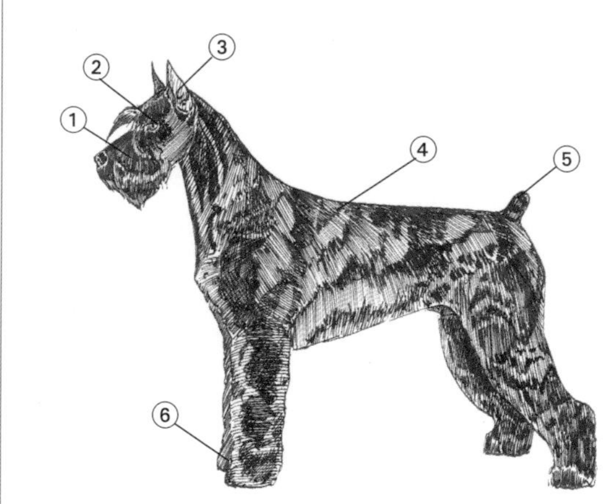

Illustrated Standard

1. Rectangular head
2. Oval deep-set eyes
3. Ears may be cropped or uncropped; when uncropped, ears are V-shaped
4. Short, straight back
5. Tail docked to second or third joint, carried high
6. Cat feet

- ❑ **Color:** solid black or pepper and salt
- ❑ **DQ:** overshot or undershot, markings other than specified

DQ = disqualified

UNDERSTANDING THE GIANT SCHNAUZER

The Giant Schnauzer is certainly not a breed for everyone. Not only is this a large and powerful dog, but it is a dog that requires a strong and consistent owner. The Giant is not for the first-time dog owner. Some say the breed is not for a dog owner that has not previously dealt with the rigors of owning a large and potentially aggressive canine.

Some breeds have been endowed by centuries of dog-breeding expertise with certain types of behavior and aptitudes. For example, terriers are very active and dig. Scent hounds are independent and follow trails. Herding dogs do best with herding jobs and will herd humans if no other stock is available. Sporting dogs are interested in hunting and retrieving. Working dogs, the group to which the Giant belongs, have been bred to function in the overall confines of a specific work role.

The Nature of the Breed

The Giant Schnauzer wants to look after its home and family. While some dogs of other breeds will fawn over any interested persons, the Giant centers on its family and its responsibilities to that family. The Giant may be somewhat aloof with strangers. Strange dogs (and other animals not part of the family circle) could attract the ire and indignation of this large and visually intimidating dog.

Some Giants are all business with people they do not know or with whom they do not feel at ease. These particular dogs do not seem to relish close contact from anyone other than their family members. These Giants tend to remain suspicious until they become convinced of the good intention of the newcomers.

Other Giants have a decidedly clownish streak that can come out at almost any time. A number of Giant Schnauzer owners have reported silly and zany behavior from their dogs when it was least expected. Visitors to a Giant's home, when these comedic outbursts occur, report how delightfully incredulous it was to see a dog with a dignified, imposing (and perhaps even a little intimidating) demeanor suddenly begin puppyish antics.

Keen intelligence, impressive physique, and unique charm have all been combined in the Giant Schnauzer.

The Various Facets

Security dogs: For a breed that was adapted to the role of security dog, the Giant Schnauzer has succeeded remarkably. While not as popular in this role in the United States as are some other breeds, the rest of the world knows and respects the Giant Schnauzer as a premier police and military dog. Many European countries actually prefer the Giant to all other such breeds. In these countries, many Giants have distinguished themselves as first-rate security/guard/protection dogs.

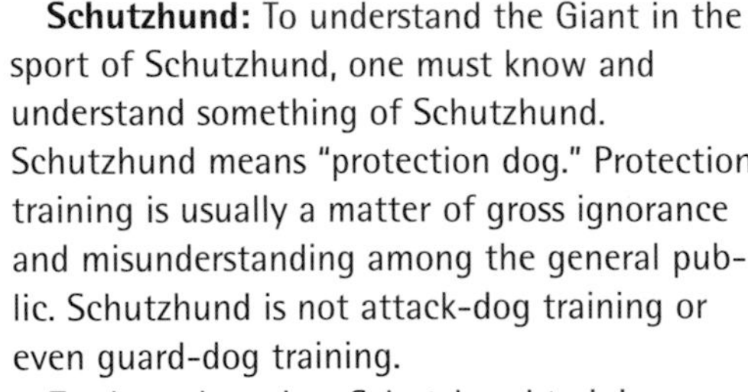

Schutzhund: To understand the Giant in the sport of Schutzhund, one must know and understand something of Schutzhund. Schutzhund means "protection dog." Protection training is usually a matter of gross ignorance and misunderstanding among the general public. Schutzhund is not attack-dog training or even guard-dog training.

To the unknowing, Schutzhund training looks like a dog trained to bite a mattress-wearing human with a heavily padded arm. While biting is a part of Schutzhund, the trained dog is *always* under control. It never bites unless the padded person initiates an attack. Then, to illustrate the great difference between a guard dog and a Schutzhund dog, the Schutzhund dog *must* stop biting on command of its owner/handler.

Schutzhund and other similar dog-training disciplines are competitions, not unlike obedience or agility events. A team composed of a dog and its handler show what they have been able to accomplish through hours and hours of diligent training based on positive reinforcement.

Contrary to popular misconception, Schutzhund dogs (including Giant Schnauzers in such training) must be approachable by strangers. After always being under control, the most important factor about Schutzhund is that a fully trained dog will always be pre-

The Giant Schnauzer made a transition from a large cattle dog to an impressive security patrol dog to special family pet. In much of Europe, the Giant is still a highly preferred police companion.

dictable. It will do what it has been trained to do only when it is given a command to do so.

Schutzhund training was originally designed for the German Shepherd Dog (GSD). Many informed canine authorities cite Schutzhund as one of the reasons that the GSD has achieved the worldwide acclaim that it has. Other dogs and dog types have become involved in this protection training. The Giant Schnauzer, like other German breeds, has done very well in Schutzhund.

Like the Giant Schnauzer as a breed, this type of training and competition is not for everyone. Schutzhund is hard work, very hard work, for the handler and for the dog. Many people and many animals are not cut out for the strenuous and demanding effort that excelling in Schutzhund will entail. It is, however, one of the fastest growing of all dog-related training activities. Once it is fully understood, Schutzhund is a very logical activity for Giants and their owners that are so inclined.

Show dogs: Dog shows are conformation competitions, sanctioned by pedigree registries called kennel clubs. Ideally, dogs are compared not against other dogs but against written blueprints for each breed (called *standards*). Standards describe each physical aspect of what the ideal or perfect dog of a particular breed should look like.

Because no absolutely perfect dog can theoretically exist, each entrant is gauged against what the standard for that breed states is ideal. These standards describe the ideal coat, color, size, physical type, and so forth. The most influential experts on that breed carefully determine standards usually over a period of years. The breed club develops the standard, which is then accepted by the registering kennel club, like the American Kennel Club (AKC), the German Kennel Club, or the Kennel Club of England.

Each country tends to have an authoritative breed club for each specific breed. This club oversees the overall breed activities and interacts with the kennel club of that specific country. In the United States, the authorizing organization for Giant Schnauzers is the Giant Schnauzer Club of America. Similar clubs exist for the Standard Schnauzer and the Miniature Schnauzer.

Local dog-fancier clubs usually conduct dog shows. These clubs contract with dog show judges, facilities, dog show contract organizations, vendors, advertising, printing, security, and other parts of the event. In the United States, dog shows regulated by the American Kennel Club have a representative of the AKC in attendance. Shows are held to a strict set of rules as are judges and exhibitors (dog owner/handlers).

In the United States, dog shows are structured around the breed categories for all dogs established by the registering organization. The American Kennel Club has seven breed-type designations called groups. The AKC accepts the following groups: sporting dogs, hounds, working dogs, terriers, toys, non-sporting dogs, and herding dogs. The AKC also recognizes a miscellaneous class for dogs seeking recognition within a specific group. The Giant and Standard Schnauzers are listed within the working group. The Miniature Schnauzer is in the terrier group.

Dog show judges are acknowledged experts on several breeds. A judge might be a specialist first in certain breeds and then, after careful

All dogs should be under the owner's control, especially large and powerful dogs like the Giant Schnauzer.

All Schnauzers will need a consistent and firm, but loving, hand.

A strong head is an asset to a good Giant.

These dogs in Germany are enroute to a Schutzhund trial.

Uncropped or cropped, moving or in repose, the Giant Schnauzer combines rugged power and an unmistakable measure of elegance in every move.

The Giant Schnauzer, in either color, attracts a lot of attention from breed fans and strangers alike.

study and classes, may be approved to judge an entire group. Most judges continue their education on the various breeds and become approved in several or all groups. Judges must be approved by the AKC in all groups before they are allowed to choose the best-in-show entrant.

Dogs, including the Giant Schnauzer, compete on an ascending scale. They are judged in their age group, their gender group, and in other in-breed categories. Ultimately, one Giant will be chosen as best of breed (BOB).

BOB winners are then combined with all the other BOB winners in their particular group. For the Giant, this will be the working group. A judge then decides the winning entrant in the working group. Group winners proceed to the best in show competition.

The motivation for most dog breeders is purely competitive. Others see seldom-realized financial possibilities of owning a winning stud dog or having quality puppies to sell as show prospects. One of the prime goals for a show dog (and its owner) is to seek a championship. A Giant seeking a championship will gain a certain number of championship points by defeating a certain number of dogs in breed judging under several different judges.

Giants generally do very well in dog shows. They are an attractive, eye-catching breed. Many Giants are said to have that often indefinable something called presence. They seem to know that they are on exhibit before the judge and project themselves even more.

Giants will require a considerable amount of grooming and training to be successful show dogs. Grooming and training cannot, however, make up for a lack of overall quality if the Giant Schnauzer does not satisfy the breed standard. Show dogs generally come from show-dog ancestry and are purchased as such, usually at a higher price than one would pay for a security dog or pet dog.

Expect a good deal of expense and time to be expended in showing one's Giant for its AKC championship. Like Schutzhund, showing one's dog may not be right for everyone. For those who find that they do like the showring, dog showing can be a very personally rewarding way of life and an excellent activity for an entire family. In many families, several generations have not only exhibited their dogs but have gone on to distinguish themselves as handlers for others and as judges.

Obedience dogs: Giant Schnauzers have done very well in the regimented training that is the obedience trial world. Obedience classes are set up in novice, open, and utility classes. Novice classes (for beginners) are the easiest. Utility classes are at the other end of the obedience spectrum and are the most advanced. To win an obedience title, a dog must earn three legs, which are awarded when the dog scores a certain number of points on each exercise and in overall competition.

In novice classes, a Giant completes basic exercises:

✔ Heeling, both on leash and without a leash,
✔ Standing for examination,
✔ Long sit,
✔ Long down, and
✔ Recall.

In the open classes, which are more advanced, a Giant would have to do

✔ Free heeling,
✔ Retrieving on the flat and over a vertical obstacle (a high jump), and
✔ A broad jump.

In the utility class, your Giant must perform advanced obedience tasks:

✔ Directed retrieval,
✔ Responding to hand signals, and
✔ Scent discrimination.

Obedience titles that can be won include:

✔ Companion Dog (C.D.) (at the novice level),
✔ Companion Dog Excellent (C.D.X.) (at the open level), and
✔ Utility Dog (U.D.) (at the utility-trial level).

In conformation dog shows, dogs that have been spayed or neutered are not eligible to compete. No such restrictions occur in obedience trials, however. Obedience trial work for your Giant Schnauzer can only make the dog a better pet. Such training is not easy for the dog or for its owner/trainer. However, there is a great thrill and a deep-seated sense of satisfaction when your dog earns an obedience title.

A bright Giant and a determined owner can garner even more titles in obedience. U.D.-titled dogs can endeavor to become obedience trial champions. There are tracking titles (in which some Giants have done very well) and herding dog titles that a Giant could attempt to earn.

Some show champions also hold obedience titles, illustrating that beauty can go with brains. A popular saying among dog fans is that the best dog has a title at both ends, for example, Champion (showring title) Barron's Typesetter of Hauppauge, U.D. (obedience title).

Family pets: For the right person, or family, the Giant Schnauzer can be a superb companion animal. Much can be said about the obvious qualities of the Giant. As mentioned, this is not a breed for everyone. The Giant may not fit every lifestyle just as every lifestyle may not fit the Giant. Because this is a large and powerful dog, it cannot be easily pulled out of the way of a speeding car as one might do with a Standard or Miniature Schnauzer. The Giant cannot be snatched up into one's arms to prevent a confrontation with a strange dog.

Most real fans of the breed, and especially the responsible Giant Schnauzer breeders, are quick to point out that this is a quick, agile, terrier-type dog in the body of a larger working breed. Many of the working-dog breeds seem to have casual, almost lazy, approaches to life. The Giant does not have such a laid-back approach. While the breed can become mellow

Left: The Giant is more than a beautiful show dog, as its athleticism demonstrates.

The Giant Schnauzer is always alert and ready for fun.

Giants need sturdy fences, strong collars and leashes, and knowledgeable owners.

Left: This pepper-and-salt Giant returns after a strenuous day in the field.

Giants love to be with their owners, and really benefit from close human companionship.

It is always good to remember that the Giant Schnauzer, like this muscular pepper-and-salt specimen, are working dogs that need appropriate exercise and activity.

When we become pet owners, we assume responsibility for all aspects of the pet's care and well-being.

A lost Giant puppy can quickly become an injured or dead Giant puppy.

at moments, perhaps many moments, the potential for quick and assertive behavior is always there.

While a Giant male dog may tolerate and even play well with smaller dogs and with females of most breeds, a large, aggressive canine stranger may be met with quid pro quo. A fight between two large dogs may not be easy to stop. Preventing such an aggressive encounter must be a top priority. Avoiding a fight may be as simple as staying away from places where other dogs are likely to be met or walking the Giant in a secure area where other potential combatants are unlikely to be seen.

The very size of the Giant is a point to be factored in when deciding whether to own a dog of this breed. Although the Giant is giant only in terms of being the largest of the Schnauzer family and not in terms of Great Danes, Mastiffs, and such, the Giant Schnauzer can be too much dog for some people to handle physically. A brawny, 6-foot (1.8-m) man may have the physical strength to extricate a Giant Schnauzer from a dangerous situation. However, a smaller man or woman, a teenager, or a senior cannot generally count on being stronger than any kind of large dog. As large dogs go, the Giant must be included among the most powerful and strongest.

While protective by nature, the Giant is an excellent indoors pet (though still large and powerful) when given proper socialization and training.

As a pet, the Giant can be very good to excellent. It is a loyal animal that strongly bonds with its family. While some Giants tend to be one-person dogs, even these are generally tolerant of others within the family circle. Some breeds can be switched around from home to home and family to family and ultimately adjust. This is not necessarily true of the Giant. It forms strong attachments to its family/pack and can really suffer when forced to leave its loved ones.

Children must be introduced to the Giant while the dog is still a puppy. Few breeds will need a more careful and concerted socialization period than the Giant Schnauzer. Exposing the Giant puppy to children and a variety of normal experiences is an important aspect of socialization.

The well-socialized Giant youngster that knows and accepts all members of its family (including the children) can become one of the best canine family members ever. This good outcome will not occur by accident. It must be structured and orchestrated.

The Giant will require time and attention on a daily basis. Most breeds will chafe if relegated to a kennel run with feeding time being the only time for human interaction. However, the Giant will do very poorly indeed if saddled with this lack of human interaction. The Giant needs regular brushing, which means a couple of times a week. Other grooming responsibilities include trimming and other hygiene requirements that must be performed quarterly. The Giant is also a very energetic and vigorous dog that must have ample exercise. This means it must have several long walks (or the equivalent) every day!

The record of the Giant as a family pet in an informed and appropriate family has produced thousands of personal accounts of great intelligence, great watchdog capacities, great prowler/burglar deterrents, and overall great pets. The potential of the Giant Schnauzer, as much as any other breed, is based on the dog-owning potential of its family. So learn about what a Giant will need from you before committing to one.

Living with a Giant Schnauzer

Giant Schnauzers are dogs that require a giant commitment on behalf of their human family. The commitment will be tested most often in the home. Day-to-day contact with a pet can allow small inconsistencies to become major problems. To all dogs, and especially to a Giant, inconsistency creates confusion. Confusion can then produce balky, stubborn behavior. Such behavior can, if left unchecked, lead to dominance issues that may not be easily resolved.

Owner Responsibilities

A dog (of any breed) that thinks it is the leader of a pack that contains humans will enforce its will on its pack members by:

✔ Reacting to perceived challenges to its leadership position;

✔ Using force to keep pack members in their appropriate places;

✔ Doing only what it wants to do when it wants to do it; and

✔ Using standard canine weaponry (its teeth) to maintain pack discipline.

Obviously, a very young Giant puppy will not be able to exhibit much in the way of dominance over its owners. However, a 90-pound (40-kg) adult can make a formidable opponent in this sad (and avoidable) power game. Puppies are little sponges that absorb much of what is going on around them. Their actions are then dictated by what they observe. If they are consistently and constantly made to feel comfortable in the bottom spot of the hierarchy, they will grow to have this as their only perspective.

One way to deal with a pet trying to move up the pack's hierarchy over some of the humans is to have all the members of the household actively involved in the raising of the puppy—in all facets of raising the puppy. Everyone feeds, walks, and helps in training. Everyone knows the rules and lives by them to the exact letter of the law. How humans respond to the dog in a particular situation does not vary. The response has been planned, and all family members must do exactly the same thing in as near to the exact same way as possible. The puppy will learn that a specific action on its part will result in a specific reaction from all the humans in the family. If all family members stay the course in teaching the young Giant in this manner, when the dog becomes an adult, it will fully understand and accept the way things are.

Giant Schnauzers and children: Many breed descriptions state unequivocally that this or that breed is "good with children." The written material about some other breeds (the Giant Schnauzer included) often adds a modifying phrase that the breed is good with children *with whom they are raised.* Care, the breed description states, must be taken to make sure that a Giant does not try to dominate young children.

Young Giants need a lot of personal attention and a lot of exercise.

As a home watchdog, the Giant excels and looks good while doing so.

General breed books have echoed this general sentiment that the Giant may try to dominate children. Some people fall back to the position that the Giant Schnauzer is excellent with children. The truth is almost certainly conditional and falls somewhere between these two blanket statements. Neither of these statements, as presented, can possibly be true in each and every situation.

Responsible Giant breeders are far closer to the truth when they say that *their* line or *their* dogs are excellent with children. Many of these breeders have decades of experience (often with their own children involved) with hundreds of Giants. They ought to know what they are talking about with *their* dogs. These responsible breeders are often willing to back up their statements with temperament guarantees to any and all purchasers of their puppies. Even so, it is highly unlikely that any breeder would make a blanket comment that *all* Giants are good with *all* children *all* the time.

Children also have to be taught the correct behaviors around all dogs and especially around their young Giant. Children are by nature inconsistent. However, they must become consistent with the puppy if they are to have the adult pet that they want.

One problem does exist that should be addressed, however. A Giant may be excellent with the children of its own family. The key question arises, though, how will it respond to visiting children? How will it respond to the horseplay, arguments, and childish squabbles that can occur between other children and children from the dog's family/pack? Even knowledgeable, longtime owners of Giants still wrestle with this quandary.

A puppy should be socialized (see "Socialization and Your Giant Schnauzer," page 50) in every possible situation. This includes when other children are visiting in the home. Again, proper socialization is a question of commitment. Parents will want their children and their Giant to interact successfully. They will also want their Giant to have a good relationship with other children. To accomplish both goals, parents must impress upon children (theirs and others) that innocent and harmless actions might appear to be something else to a Giant.

This is the very reason that homes with very young children (probably those under ages 10 or even 12) are not good candidates for owning a Giant Schnauzer. Some immature children might even provoke a hostile response from another child in order to demonstrate their dog's protective ability. That could be a very frightening scenario.

Giant Schnauzers and other dogs: There are no absolutes about Giants interacting with other dogs. Some very large, very intimidating Giants have been great companions to other dogs in their families. The added phrase "dogs that they have been raised with" appears in many breed discussions about Giants and other dogs in a home. Dogs that live in a home together generally work out their own rules and their own détente. Families do have to be careful if they favor one dog over the other. Doing so can cause jealous reactions in some dogs, including Giants.

As with children, the question arises about how a Giant responds to dogs that are not in its family and to strange dogs and strays. Many Giants do very well with small dogs and dogs of the opposite gender. A male Giant Schnauzer confronted by an aggressive male dog may do what you would expect a protective dog from a drover background to do. Unless restrained, the Giant will attack and use its terrier-like speed and large body size to best the challenger. Because of the potential damage that a Giant could do to most other dogs in such a confrontation, Giant owners must foresee and anticipate dangerous situations and avoid them as much as possible.

Giant Schnauzers and other pets: The terrier aspects of the Giant's genetic heritage often win out with some Giants and make them a real threat to cats and other small pets. Many terriers have a prey drive that virtually turns them into the vermin attacker of their earlier centuries.

Established cats can learn to avoid a clumsy Giant puppy and come to a shaky but reasonable armed truce as the youngster grows up. Adequate evidence seems to indicate, though, that bringing a cat into the established home of a Giant is unwise.

The same could be said for releasing ferrets, rabbits, guinea pigs, and other small animals near a Giant Schnauzer (or almost any terrier). Members of this breed can have considerable prey drive and would probably make short work of any small animal intruders into their domains. Why take a

Owning a Giant should be a family obligation and responsibility. It is important that the dog always know that it is below all the humans in the family in the pack hierarchy.

Responsible Giant owners make certain that legitimate strangers in the home are not met alone by a dog that has home protection as a high priority.

chance that a Giant would act like countless other dogs would?

Giant Schnauzers and strangers: A family committed to owning a Giant Schnauzer must take reasonable precautions to avoid incidents between a protective Giant and human strangers trespassing onto the dog's turf. As with children, other dogs, and other pets, these reasonable precautions begin with thorough socialization (especially within the young dog's own home) and continued training.

One would not want to try to do a frontal lobotomy on a Giant Schnauzer to make such a dog ignore strangers. Neither would one want to put meter readers, postal workers, and innocent strangers into danger simply by coming into your yard or home. Many Giants must be crated, kenneled, or put into another room when strangers are in the home for the first time. Other Giants can be trained to accept (however grudgingly) the presence of guests that have the approval of the dog's family. A Giant that persists in threatening behavior toward a guest or invited stranger should be placed where it cannot be a threat.

Caring for Your Giant Schnauzer

Many experts on this breed continue to stress emphatically that the Giant must have close, daily contact with its human family/pack members. That such a large and powerful dog should be largely an inside pet is decidedly true. That the Giant will benefit markedly from being near its humans during most of its waking hours is also true. For whatever else the Giant Schnauzer may be, it is a people-oriented dog. Without close association with human beings, the Giant is rudderless. It has no fulcrum upon which to balance its instincts. Such a dog is a real liability to itself, to other dogs, and to people.

The Right Environment

The home of the Giant should certainly have a place that is uniquely and specifically for the dog. A cage, crate, or carrier can be your Giant's den (see page 43). Fences around yards should be strong and tall. A Giant Schnauzer loose in a suburban neighborhood is, at the very least, a potential lawsuit.

While it is possible that some Giant owners make use of outside runs with doghouses, the conventional Giant wisdom goes against this thinking. A Giant expelled from being near its humans, even for only a brief time, could become brokenhearted and even resentful.

Exercise

One part of the commitment that comes with owning a Giant Schnauzer is the willingness to take the dog for long walks, runs, or other physical activity more than once each day. The Giant has great energy. This energy must be channeled in the right way or it will indubitably come out in a wrong way. Giants need long walks or runs every day. The more consistent the time, frequency, and duration of exercise periods are, the better things will be with the dog. Appropriate amounts of regular exercise will be reflected in many other areas of a Giant's life.

A well-exercised dog will be far less prone to boredom and potential destructiveness than an animal receiving too little physical activity. Exercise will often reap benefits in easier training. Tired dogs and puppies sleep better in the night and are less apt to cry or whine in their crates. Better eating habits can stem from hunger brought on by enough physical activity. Well-exercised Giants seem to be less stressed and better adjusted to their entire home situation.

You should always keep in mind that the Giant is not listed in the working group by accident. The genetic heritage of this breed traces directly to dogs that paid their way by doing hard work driving livestock or serving as guard dogs. To ignore this ancestry is to attempt to remold the Giant into a couch potato, something that it clearly is not.

Some forms of exercise—Schutzhund, agility, flyball, obedience, and the like—combine mental stimulation with physical activity. These events are good for both canines and humans and seem especially important for a large and very active Giant Schnauzer.

Traveling

Some breeds make better travelers than others. Schnauzer authorities have mixed attitudes about Giants and mobility. Some people hold

When traveling with a pet, the first consideration should be the safety and comfort of the animal.

that the Giant is better left at home and that exposure to many strangers is traumatic to the dog. Others believe that Giants make excellent road warriors.

The matter of owner and family commitment to the Giant applies in any discussion of traveling. Two considerations actually work against each other in regard to traveling with a Giant.

✔ First, the Giant can be so bonded to its human or humans that time away is very stressful for the dog. Therefore, traveling with the dog is what the dog would seem to want.

✔ Second, the Giant Schnauzer is very much a creature of consistency and habit, preferring things to be the same. Therefore, the dog would probably prefer not to travel.

So should you travel with your Giant? Only you, as a committed and responsible owner, can answer that question for you and your pet.

If you do travel with your Giant, remember that unrestrained dogs or puppies in an automobile can become the cause of an accident. Either put your pet into a carrier, secure it with a seat belt especially designed for canines, or leave the pet at home. Traveling with a Giant Schnauzer should be a pleasure, not a fearsome liability. For specifics about bringing your new puppy home, see page 46.

HOW-TO: GROOMING YOUR

Your Giant Schnauzer will need regular grooming. The extent of this grooming depends on what you want to do with your Giant. A show dog will definitely need far more detailed grooming than will a pet, obedience, security, or Schutzhund dog. The grooming needs of some dogs, like the Beagle or Basenji, are minimal. Other breeds, like the Keeshond, the Old English Sheepdog, and Puli, need a great deal of grooming. The time needed for grooming should be factored into your decision to purchase a Giant and the commitment that must be made to keep a Giant looking like a Giant.

The Giant Schnauzer has a double coat. The outside coat is a hard, weather-repellant brush of guard hairs. You can take two approaches when dealing with the outer coat of your Giant Schnauzer.

1. Either you or a groomer could clip your pet's coat every six to eight weeks.

2. You could learn to hand strip the dog's coat.

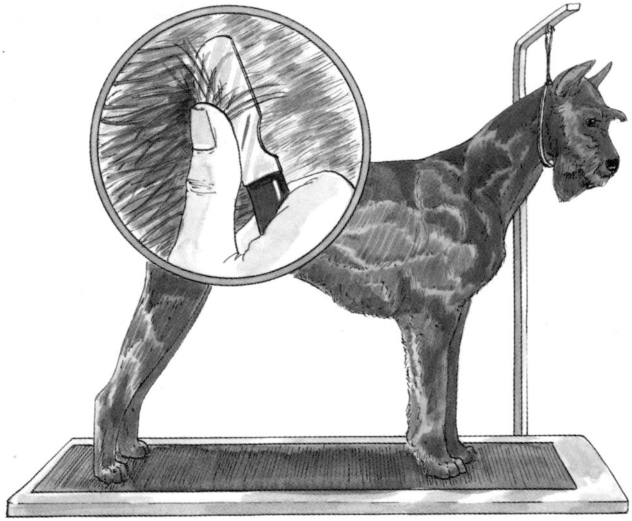

To look their best, Giant Schnauzers require regular grooming in the form of "hand stripping" the coat (see inset). Stripping is often time-consuming, but it keeps the dog in the traditional Schnauzer "hard coat," which is lost when the dog is clipped.

Both approaches have positive and negative aspects. The following describes these in detail.

✔ Clipping your Giant's coat, especially if the dog is not going to be shown in the ring, is quicker. However, the coat becomes very soft. A soft coat is completely alien to the character of the Giant Schnauzer.

✔ Softness is a characteristic of the near-kin breed Bouvier des Flandres. Clipping, in the words of one Giant fan, "will take all the character out of the appearance of the dog, and is just not for the showring."

✔ Clipping is easier and is done by Giant breeders for old dogs and dogs never to be shown in public again.

✔ Giant Schnauzer stripping is not a task that many neighborhood groomers like to do. One of the humorous questions asked of Giant Schnauzer owners is if their dog is a giant Scottish Terrier. While funny on the surface, the question makes a valid point in that grooming for the short-legged Scottie is quite similar to that of the Giant. Their head shape is very similar, and their beard and eyebrows can look much the same. Even the hard coat of the smaller dog is stripped in the same general manner as the Giant's coat is stripped.

✔ Stripping is hard work and is performed without any mechanical devices (no clippers and no scissors).
✔ Stripping will not be cheap, even if you can find a groomer who knows how to do it correctly.
✔ Hand stripping the coat is a long and laborious procedure in which the hard Schnauzer outer coat must be plucked. It should be done either quarterly or twice a year (depending on the hardness of the specific Giant's coat).
✔ By stripping, the dead hair is actually plucked out. This leaves the coat with the hard wire texture that adds so much to the appearance of the Giant Schnauzer.

Even with the obvious differences between having a Giant clipped and having the dog stripped, stripping seems far and away to be better in keeping with the spirit of the breed. Part of the allure of the Giant Schnauzer is its toughness. When comparing the Giant with the Bouvier, one of them looks like a big teddy bear and the other looks like an elegant and powerful guard dog. Want to guess which one is clipped and which one is hand stripped? Want to guess which breed is which?

Whatever coat-grooming choice you make, your Giant will still need some other grooming done. Several areas are important for any dog of this breed that spends a lot of time in close proximity to humans:

1. The beard of your Giant should be washed almost every day to remove leftover food remnants.

2. The beard and face should be brushed daily.

3. The coat should be brushed with a hard-bristled brush twice each week.

4. The hindquarters and the male Giant's genitals should be sponged off to remove any bits of fecal material or urine stain or smell.

As with so many other aspects of pet owning, grooming is best begun very early in the life of a Giant Schnauzer. A small puppy that learns to enjoy being brushed and handled will be much easier to groom when it is an adult.

5. Baths, especially if dry baths or bath wipes are used every other week or so, do not have to occur more than every six weeks for a Giant. Bathing a dog too frequently can dry out its skin and coat.

6. Start early with a Giant to give its teeth regular (at least weekly) attention. Regular brushing, combined with dental attention by your veterinarian, will help keep your pet's teeth white and its breath bearable.

7. The toenails of a Giant that does not typically walk or run on hard or paved surfaces will need regular attention. Start early. Carefully clip off sharp points (avoiding the quick), and control nail growth with a nail file.

8. Check your Giant's eyes and ears daily, especially if your pet has access to woods and lawns. Briers and other foreign objects can injure these delicate sense organs.

INTRODUCING A GIANT SCHNAUZER INTO YOUR HOME

Long before you ever bring your young Giant home, you have a considerable amount of work to do. You must prepare your home for its new occupant.

Before You Buy a Giant Schnauzer

A breed mentor is that unique individual who wants to help people considering his or her breed to have the most successful outcome possible. As such, a Giant Schnauzer breed mentor will be willing to tell a person or a family that the Giant may not be right for them. A mentor, usually a breeder of Giants, will be willing to send a prospective purchaser to someone else for a puppy if the mentor does not have just the right Giant.

Finding a Breed Mentor

You, as a potential Giant owner, will have to put in some effort to find a Giant mentor. There are enough responsible and responsive breeders, however, that a dedicated search should turn up several possible mentors. The job then becomes one of convincing a busy breeder that you (and your family) are really worthy candidates for owning a Giant Schnauzer and that mentoring you is not a waste of time.

Visit dog shows, especially those in your geographic area, to meet individuals exhibiting their Giants. Talk with as many fans of this breed as possible. Go on the Internet and absorb all you can about Giants and their various aspects and activities. Listen and remember the names of people who are respected among their peers within the breed.

A breed mentor should prove invaluable to you. Find someone you can trust and then follow what he or she suggests. If you have found the right mentor, your chances of finding the right puppy are greatly enhanced and your chances of fulfilling your commitment to this puppy are much more likely.

Decide whether a large and active dog will fit your lifestyle before you consider purchasing or adopting a Giant.

Finding an experienced Giant Schnauzer person to mentor you and your ownership of your Giant will help you avoid the pitfalls that are so often encountered by novices in this breed.

Before the Search

Defining what you are seeking: With a breed expert assisting you as a mentor, you can now decide what aspects of the Giant Schnauzer are important to you. Perhaps you think showing your dog would be a good activity for you and your family. Participating in obedience trials (since your Giant will require extensive, professional training anyway) may be something to consider. Perhaps all you want is a well-trained pet.

Now is the time to decide what you want in a Giant. You must know what you really want and what you can realistically hope to achieve before you can really start the search for your Giant. Because of the versatility of the breed, you have several options. Generally, dogs that will have certain abilities are from a family of dogs that excel at those abilities. Show dogs come from show lines, Schutzhund dogs generally come from Schutzhund lines, and so forth. Knowing what you want will greatly dictate where you can seek it.

Preparing for your search: Finding a breed mentor has actually been a trial run and great background for your quest for the right Giant for you and your family. In fact, your mentor may have just the dog you are seeking. Even if the mentor does not, your preparation has given you a base of information not only about the breed but also about breeders. This information will be very valuable at this time.

Breed magazines, videos, books, and other materials are available that will help you locate potential sources for your Giant. You can plan trips to significant Giant Schnauzer events and visit kennels in other parts of the country. You can search the Internet and see what litters are planned and where they are.

One rule is definitely true. The more you prepare, the easier your search will ultimately be. This preparation phase is another great way to involve your family. A Giant that results from careful planning and family discussions is coming into a much better setting than one just bought spontaneously.

Searching for the Right Giant

After you have found a breed mentor, have decided what you want, and have prepared for the search, you have all the tools to seek out and find the right Giant. This part may entail visiting a number of kennels that specialize in the kind of Giant Schnauzer you want. Depending on what criteria and standards you have set for your prospective Giant, your search may be over quickly or it may take months.

You may have decided that you want a salt-and-pepper female from a line strong in obedience work. Several pups may meet these requirements, but they may not be for sale or may have already been sold. You may even have to go onto a waiting list (or waiting lists) and pay a deposit for an as-yet-unborn puppy.

A puppy or an older dog: In some breeds, this is really a quandary. The Giant Schnauzer is a bit different. Because many Giants are not necessarily good with children that they have not been around all their lives, a puppy is really a much better choice for a family with children or with the prospect of children.

An adult Giant could easily enter a new home of a single individual or couple, but that would depend largely on the ability for the dog and people to bond with each other. Some adult dogs just will not bond with some new owners (and the reverse is true). Finding the right adult, through breed rescue or through a breeder, will depend on many variables. An adult Giant may be perfect for a committed individual, but a family with children should choose a puppy.

Puppy Proofing

Your yard: If you have a yard in which your Giant can play, you have several tasks before it will be truly safe for your pet. Puppy proofing is also a great way to involve your family in welcoming the new puppy. Children make great detectives in searching out the most basic, and yet often the most overlooked, dangers that may be found in your environment. Enlist their enthusiastic participation. You and your children should get down to the puppy's level (on hands and knees) in order to spot potential dangers not seen from adult height.

Carefully check your fence for weaknesses, holes, and places that can be easily jumped over, pushed through, or dug under. If you do not have a fence, then you should have a strong and high (6 feet [1.8 m] minimum) one built *prior* to bringing your Giant Schnauzer home.

Puppy proofing is simply searching for those things that could potentially bring harm to your Giant puppy. Children can often perform this task very well by being able to get down on the floor and looking over, under, around, through, and behind for dangerous items and situations.

Look for the very best possible Giant when you decide to purchase one.

Check the fence itself for safety features. Do the gates shut (and stay shut) securely?

Make a careful inventory of what plants and shrubs you have in your yard or in adjacent flower beds. Some plants, like azaleas and philodendrons, may make a chewing puppy very ill. (Your county cooperative extension agent can provide you with a complete list of plants that are normally grown in your geographic locale. Be aware of any toxic flowers and shrubs growing off your property that your puppy can get into. You should also check your garden and yard for any wild-occurring flora that might harm your puppy. For example, pets can often touch poison oak or poison ivy (and even spread the sap and the rash to you). Mistletoe and many fungi are also poisonous to your pet.

Look around your yard for bushes and trees with sharply broken branches. Search for sharp, pointed objects. These could cause serious eye damage to a young dog. Fill in holes into which a running pet might step.

You should also look at precariously balanced items (birdbaths are an example) that could turn over and injure or kill your new pet. Check any features of your yard, like walls, from which a puppy could fall and be injured.

If you have a swimming pool or a decorative fishpond, these must be fenced. An unwatched puppy, in only a moment, could topple in, be unable to get out, and drown.

Before you bring a Giant into your home, be certain that you have a safe place for such a dog to live.

Decide what you want your Giant to be: a show dog, an obedience dog, or a Schutzhund dog.

Your garage or carport is no place for your Giant, either as a puppy or an adult. The danger of accidents or chemical spills in such areas make them taboo for pets.

Your home: Because a large part of the commitment that must be made to a Giant Schnauzer involves keeping the puppy (and later the adult dog) near you, you must carefully check for and clear the interior of your home of potential harm. Again, the children in a family can prove of great value when puppy proofing from down where puppies view things. Although puppy proofing each home is different, you can follow some basic beginning points.

✔ Search every floor surface—carpet, tile, and hardwood—for tiny things that may have been dropped and overlooked. Needles, pins, map tacks, overlooked broken glass fragments, and other ordinary items could be swallowed and do severe, often fatal damage to a puppy.

✔ Take special notice of any and all rooms where a young dog could go. Check these areas for any items that could hurt the youngster. Look for dropped medications, pest control baits or traps, and again for hurtful sharp things.

✔ Small toys, and other discarded or forgotten items, in children's rooms (or rooms that once were children's rooms) can do great damage to the puppy that swallows them.

✔ Sponges, cleaning cloths, and cleaning solutions in kitchens, laundry rooms, and bathrooms (places where puppies are often confined during the housebreaking process) are especially harmful to the health of a puppy; some are even fatal.

✔ Garbage pails and wastebaskets can contain discards that could entice a puppy and hurt it. Care must always be taken to protect a curious puppy from the things that you have thrown away.

✔ As in other parts of the environment, dangerous places might exist as well as dangerous things. Tight squeezes behind furniture and appliances can entrap and traumatize a young puppy. Falls from balconies, stairwells, and porches could injure young animals. Puppies can get their inquisitive heads caught in places that you might never dream would be possible.

✔ Puppy proofing also requires you review daily household activities. Make sure they do not allow a young Giant to escape outside. Remembering to close doors and gates should be part of the total family commitment to owning a Giant Schnauzer.

✔ Other regular household actions could be unsafe for a puppy. Slammed doors, unthinking steps, even careless play could injure a little canine. Part of puppy proofing is to know and remember when the puppy is not in its crate or exercise pen and act wisely for the good of the pet.

Going Home

The trip home: The best way, the safest way, and the least traumatic way to bring your new pet home is for you to go and bring it home yourself. Not only are you sure that you are getting the puppy that you bargained for, your puppy will have some opportunity to learn about you as you bring it to your home.

Sometimes the distance may be great and a longer drive is necessary. Other times you may have found a breeder with just the right puppy very near you. In either case, the trip home needs your full attention and careful planning. This will be the first time that you and your puppy have been together for any length of time. It is important your lives together get off to a good start.

If your trip is of several hours' duration or more, using a travel carrier will be a good idea. Your new pup will have a secure place in which to ride. If the carrier is to serve as the dog's den when it arrives home, the introduction process will have already begun. Securely fasten the carrier to a car seat belt in the backseat of the car.

Later, you may want to let your Giant Schnauzer travel with a seat belt designed specifically for dogs. For this first trip, though, a carrier is best. The carrier needs to be near someone that can look in on the puppy and perhaps say some soothing words. The carrier will need a soft liner or some old towels to make the trip more comfortable. It is not necessary (or advisable) to put food and water into the carrier, as this will generally cause a big mess and a wet puppy.

If your trip is a long one, plan to stop at least every hour to give the puppy a break and a little water. Pack some bottled water and some of the same food that the puppy ate at its original home. Pet stores, catalogs, and online e-commerce companies may have water and food bowls that can be used specifically for traveling. Some of these will suit the needs of your new puppy. Remove the pup from the carrier and put on a leash and collar (which should not be kept on a dog or puppy while in a carrier or crate). While securely attached to the leash, you can give the puppy a chance to relieve itself before returning it to the carrier to resume the trip home.

When you walk your young puppy, do not walk the youngster where other dogs have been. Adult dogs can carry diseases even if they themselves do not have them. Your puppy will not be immunized against these possible diseases until it has had all shots at about 14 weeks of age. Until that time, do not utilize the dog walks at highway rest areas or the places used commonly in front of pet stores or veterinary clinics. Pick out new territory for your puppy in order to avoid coming into contact with some life-threatening ailment spread from someone else's pet.

Initial home phases: Upon reaching your home (even before you go inside), go immediately to the predesignated area in your yard

One of the most essential pieces of pet-owning equipment is the cage or crate. Shown here is a young Giant safely behind a pet gate in an easily cleaned laundry room, with containers for food and water and the pup's home-within-your-home, its crate.

that you have chosen to be your pup's waste relief spot. This should be a specific location—a bush, a rock, or something readily identifiable by sight to the young dog. Wait patiently and somberly there for the puppy to relieve itself. When it eventually does (and it will), praise the puppy enthusiastically and then go immediately into your puppy-proofed home with its newest occupant.

Though you may be very proud of your Giant puppy, wait several days before you invite in hordes of friends and neighbors to meet it. These first days will be a very traumatic time for the youngster. Lots of new faces will only make things more difficult for a bewildered pup.

A new puppy after a long trip will be tired and ready for sleep. While you and your family may want to play with the weary youngster, give the puppy time to rest. This is also a good time to introduce the pup to its new home within your home—the carrier or crate where it will sleep and spend some quality personal time.

Your Giant's Den— An Essential

Crate training: Giant Schnauzer authorities and general canine experts agree that your new pet should be crate trained. Crate training involves the use of a cage, crate, or carrier as a den for your Giant. There are many excellent reasons to crate train your pet and only erroneous reasons not to do so:

Crate training (the general phrase used for this activity) makes use of some deeply ingrained canine instincts to help make your pet a better companion animal.

Canines, wild and domestic, are denning creatures. They will seek a place in which to sleep, rest, and relax. Dens or lairs are the homes of wolves, coyotes, dingos, and feral dogs (dogs of domestic canine heritage that are living in the wild).

Pet dogs without formal crate training will still usually find some less preferable place within a home to serve as a lair or den. This might be under a bed, in a closet, or in a remote corner. This location will become, with varying degrees of success, the dog's place of refuge, relaxation, and safety.

By crate training, you can structure this natural desire to have a den into a great way to keep your Giant, first as a puppy and then as an adult, in one place and under your supervision (an important aspect of your commitment to a Giant Schnauzer).

As a large and protective dog, times will arise when you will want to temper your Giant's natural guard-dog tendencies. When this occurs, you can place the dog into its crate.

Your Giant should sleep in its crate from the first night on through the rest of its life. Many pet owners think that sharing their beds with a puppy is a cute and loving thing to do. You should not do this for many reasons: transmission of disease (in both directions), sharing of parasites, and so on. A major reason for a Giant Schnauzer owner never to start this is that a 20-pound (9-kg) puppy can grow to be a 90-pound (40-kg) adult that may not want to change sleeping arrangements when it has outgrown your bed.

Your dog's crate should *never* be used as punishment. The crate is a place where everything is calm and good, not a prison. Every correctly crate-trained dog will often choose to enter its crate at its own volition when it wants to nap or when things have been a little stressful.

Another canine instinct is present in crate training. In the dens and lairs of wild canines and in the litter pens of domesticated dogs, pups are trained by their mothers not to make messes. The age-old reason for this training and the instincts behind it stem from the fact that mother canines often had to hunt for food. In so doing, they left their offspring unattended and unguarded. Strong fecal and urine odors would draw predators to the den and its helpless baby inhabitants. Because most puppies want to avoid fouling where they sleep, crate training thus becomes one of the greatest aids in housebreaking your new Giant. While a puppy may make mistakes, even in its crate, this instinct will encourage it to defecate and urinate at the outside location chosen by you previously.

The crate is not a holding tank or cell for a dog or puppy. No pet should be left for more than a few hours in its crate, except during the night when you want to control a young Giant's unsupervised movements while you are sleeping. Crates can be used in combination with other confinement approaches that will contain the youngster without depriving it of water, toys, and limited (but safeguarded) mobility.

A crate, with its door left open, could be placed into a kitchen, a large bathroom, or a laundry room. The activities of a puppy in one of these easily cleaned areas can be further restricted by placing the crate into a portable dog pen that can be quickly erected in the center of the room.

Your Giant will want to be protector and guard over all that you possess.

Far from being a prison or cell, a cage or carrier will become a dog's own special "den," or place, of its own.

A collapsible gate can be placed across a door to keep a puppy inside a laundry room or bathroom and still allow the youngster visual access to adjacent areas. Such gates can also be used to keep puppies away from unsafe areas in a home.

Crate types: You have two main options for crates that will be used as a den. First, you can use the airline style carrier (like the one you may have used to bring your Giant puppy home). It is a fiberglass box (put together in two parts) with ventilation and a see-through, heavy-gauge steel, wire door. One advantage of this type of enclosure for your dog's crate is that it can double as a carrier if and when you travel with your Giant. A carrier is quite strong and sturdy. Another advantage is that the inside of a carrier is dark and more denlike.

Your second option is to use an actual crate. This is a wire enclosure (often black or silver in color) that ranges in size to fit all breeds. A crate has the advantage of being completely collapsible. It is lighter than a carrier and may not be quite as sturdy. It offers the advantages of an airy design that allows more ventilation and light into the area where your pet has its den. It can be placed into the back of a van or station wagon for trips, but it is not as portable as a carrier.

Crate size: Both crates and carriers are very satisfactory for the purposes for which they are intended. It is important that when you choose either of these options that you choose one for the size of the *adult* that your puppy will become. Giants grow rapidly, and they can outgrow small crates seemingly overnight. Buy for the future, and buy only once!

An important point to make about purchasing an adult-sized carrier or crate is that you must keep the area within the enclosure appropriate for the size of the puppy as it grows. If a puppy is placed into an adult-sized crate, it may find that the far back corner of the crate would be an appropriate place to relieve itself because it does not sleep there. Give the puppy just enough room in which to turn around and to sleep comfortably, and the crate will function as it should.

To enlarge the crate area available to the puppy as it grows, you can use a partition kit. These are available at many pet supply stores. A partition kit allows you to keep the inside area appropriate for the size of your growing Giant.

Crates are an important advance in having a dog live in your home near to you. Your Giant will, if given the right training, come to love and depend on its crate. The Giant will benefit mentally and physically from having a place of its own within your busy household. Many dog experts stress the overwhelming positives of crate training for dogs that share their owners' homes.

Giant Schnauzers do not do well as kennel or backyard dogs isolated from the humans that they love. Most responsible Giant breeders would never dream of selling one of their dogs to a home that would banish a pet to the backyard, away from the human contact it so craves.

Adjustment Time

Your Giant puppy, as will all puppies, will need some time to feel at home and to fit into your family and lifestyle. Remember that this is a shock to the pup. Yesterday, it was happy in the only world it had ever known, with mother and littermates. Today, the young dog is with you and your family in a strange, new world.

Simply bringing a puppy into your home and ignoring it is quite inconsiderate and very unwise. A puppy will need a new pack to join. That pack will now be your family. Learning what the rules are will take even a smart pup, like your Giant, some time. Do all you can to help shorten that time by being aware of the stresses and strains that your Giant is going through.

A responsible person must see that the pup goes outside to the relief spot when it needs to and that it is appropriately praised and reinforced for relieving itself in the right place. This responsible person will also give appropriate dog food and clean water to the young Giant, play with the puppy, and clean up any messes. Having someone near it much of the day will dramatically help the youngster become acclimatized to its new home.

The Giant's First Night in Its New Home

All members of the pup's household have to agree with how the Giant's sleeping arrangements will be handled. If one person in the family breaks the routine, the training of the puppy will suffer. All family members should agree on the following points.

✔ The puppy sleeps in its crate at night and nowhere else!

✔ No person in the family hears the plaintive cries and whines of the lonely youngster and goes to "rescue" it from its crate!

You can, however, help the puppy get through the first few nights in its crate. First, plan ahead and put a toy or a piece of bedding (or something with the scent of its mother and littermates) into the crate. This will give a smell of home to the place.

Second, place the crate where the pup realizes that its new family is not very far away. This location should be far enough away so that sleeping humans are not kept awake all night by the cries of the puppy.

Third, an old ticking (not electric) clock near the crate was once considered a good way to give a puppy the sensation of nearness. This still works (be sure the alarm is in the off position). However, a small radio tuned very low to an all-night talk radio station can give the puppy the faint sounds of humans that can be comforting. The radio must not be placed into the crate, but nearby.

The Giant may need a few nights to understand that it is safe in its new home and to forget its littermates and mother. However, if the rules are patiently followed, it will surely do so.

Housebreaking

Because of the breed's brightness, the way that the puppy is housebroken must be done the same way each time. If any variation on the method used occurs, the dog will file that information away as an inconsistency for use at a later time. Until all persons in the family learn the procedure individually, all persons in the family should go out with the puppy to the relief spot and learn as the puppy learns.

There are three main elements in housebreaking: crate training, going outside to the same relief place, and ridding the home of the hidden scent of mistakes. Each of these elements depends on the other two. Without all three, housebreaking efforts will probably fail with the Giant.

Crate training has already been discussed in this chapter. It will play a major role in housebreaking. Here are some suggestions about using a crate as a housebreaking aid.

First, as early as possible each morning, remove the puppy or dog from the crate to make a trip to the relief area. Second, as late as possible each night, take the puppy outside to the relief area. Then place it into the crate and go to bed. Third, if a mistake occurs in the crate, thoroughly clean up the mess, remove and replace any affected bedding, and then spray the area where the mistake occurred with a dog odor neutralizer (with enzymes) made specifically for this purpose.

Going outside to the same place: Dogs are scenting creatures. Canine scenting ability plays the key role in housebreaking. If a dog owner correctly uses this canine scenting ability, a puppy can learn exactly where its relief spot is and what it should do there.

✔ Choose a relief spot that is near enough to visit conveniently in bad weather, out of regular foot traffic, and clearly defined by some specific object (a bush, a stump, or a rock).

✔ Impress upon the puppy that potty time is not play time. Use a collar and leash to take the young Giant out to the relief area, even if it is in your own fenced backyard. The collar and leash become a signal that relief time has arrived.

✔ As you go out to the relief site, be somber and quiet. Do not be cheerfully talking to the puppy (as you might during playtime). If you say

CHECKLIST

Housebreaking Do's and Don'ts

✔ Don't swat a puppy with a rolled-up newspaper, your hand, or anything else when it makes a mess inside. The youngster will not have full bladder control until it is about six months old and is probably piddling where it made a previous mistake. Swatting a puppy that cannot have any idea why the boss is striking it confuses the puppy. Such corporal punishment could lead to fear and resentment.

✔ Don't rub a puppy's nose into its own excrement (you will not be able to do this to an adult Giant Schnauzer). This is another pointless gesture that goes right over the puppy's head and leaves you with a dirty and smelly puppy.

✔ Don't shout and throw things when a puppy starts making a mess inside. Clap your hands or do something to break the pup's train of thought. Pick up the youngster and rush it out to the relief site. Go through the process as if it were a regular relief break.

✔ Do regulate the time your puppy eats, and take the pup out immediately thereafter. You should feed it several small meals a day instead of keeping a full food bowl unavailable at all times.

✔ Do be alert to signs that your pet wants to go outside. Staying near the door, having an anxious look on its face, sniffing around and going in circles, and coming to you and then going back to the door are all signs that a pet wants to do what you have taught it to do.

✔ Do always praise the puppy when it goes where it should. Your Giant will live for this reinforcing praise. This will also help it do what it should do where it is supposed to do it.

✔ Do have your entire family follow the exact same model as you do in housebreaking.

✔ Do understand that Giants will learn rapidly but that consistently continuing the housebreaking steps will help the pet continue doing the right things.

✔ Do use puppy pads in the area near the crate (in the laundry room, bathroom, or kitchen) for a very young puppy, a sick pet, or a very old dog. So-called paper training is a stopgap measure at best. It creates confusion for a puppy in that there are now *two* right places to go.

anything at all, say it in stern and serious tones. The intelligent Giant will quickly pick up on your mood. After the puppy has relieved itself at the right place, then you can praise the puppy immediately and vigorously. Then be quiet again, go back inside, and return the pup to its crate. Wait a few minutes before you release the young dog from the crate for playtime.

Getting all the scent of mistakes out: This element of housebreaking may seem to be the simplest, but it is not. It may seem to be of minor importance, but it ranks with the other two as being of great importance. Remember that your Giant Schnauzer is a scenting animal. It can detect smells that no human ever could. The average pet owner gets only the first layer of odor of urine or feces out from the place where a mistake has occurred. Cleaning with disinfectants at this level may be a comfort to the humans that live there, but it actually has little effect on the pet.

Do not just clean the surface smell (the ones that humans can detect). Use an enzymatic odor neutralizer. Several products use enzymes to do away with urine and fecal smells from a pet's mistake. They can be obtained at pet supply stores and at some veterinarians. Thoroughly spray this neutralizer on the mistake, and rest assured that the enzymes have erased this one wrong spot.

Hard work never hurt a Giant Schnauzer and helps use up excess energy.

It is important to socialize a Giant with any animals that it may encounter.

HOW-TO: SOCIALIZE YOUR

Socialization and Your Giant Schnauzer

Socialization simply means allowing your Giant puppy to meet and become comfortable with as many people, and situations, as possible under controlled conditions. As a puppy encounters people of all sizes, shapes, and colors, it will learn not to fear the differences that may be a part of its life for a long time. The same thing is true of situations that may confront a Giant in its life with you in the future.

Why Is Socialization Important?

Without socialization, the work that most dogs do in connection with humankind would be greatly limited or impossible. Socializing gives a very young dog an opportunity to experience vastly different events, people, and situations under the watchful and comforting eye of its owner. The goal is a confident dog that remains alert to all possible dangers or problems but that does not overreact to the mundane or usual.

Why Is Socialization Crucial for a Giant Schnauzer?

Some people may see the Giant as an identical personality to the Miniature Schnauzer but in the large, economy size. The only common ancestor that both these breeds share is the Standard Schnauzer.

It is crucial that you socialize your young Giant puppy by taking the youngster out to experience new sights, sounds, smells, and different situations. A puppy thus socialized will become a reliable adult dog that can safely go anywhere and everywhere.

Nowadays, connection is a real genetic stretch. The Standard and the Giant share some general work-related background. The Miniature and the Standard share much of the same companion pet capabilities. The distance in makeup and background between the Miniature and the Giant Schnauzers, however, is fairly large.

The difference in the need and type of socialization necessary for the Giant in relation to that for the Miniature can be illustrated mathematically. A good average size for an adult Miniature Schnauzer is 13 inches (33 cm) tall (measured at the shoulder) with a weight of 15 pounds (7 kg). An adult male Giant may be 27 inches (69 cm) tall and weigh 90 pounds (40 kg). Thus the Giant usually stands twice as tall and weighs six times as much!

If the breeds were identical except for height and weight, the socialization needs would still be different because a large dog cannot be simply picked up by its owner when potential trouble comes around. The fact that the Giant has become one of the premier protection/law enforcement/military dogs in history while the lap-pet qualities of the Miniature have been heightened and emphasized gives the reader a more realistic view and a different prospective on socialization needs.

Every Giant must be thoroughly socialized and thoroughly trained. Without a real commitment to these two tasks by a prospective owner, the Giant should *not* be purchased. To entertain a mental picture of the Giant as just a bigger version of the Miniature in personality, as it is in appearance, is an error.

Socialization is another place where an entire family can get involved. Enlist the whole family group in mapping out as many possible circumstances that a pet of yours (in your lifestyle and special circumstances) might have to face. Some such circumstances for an average family might include the following:

✔ You have friends that are frail and walk with canes or walkers (or people in wheelchairs) that might be frightening to a young puppy.

✔ You want to walk your Giant in a public park where you might encounter crowds and loud and unusual (for your regular lifestyle) noises.

✔ Your children are all teenagers, and you want your Giant Schnauzer to be good around younger children as well.

✔ Your children are all boys (or girls), and you want interaction with both genders to feel natural to the Giant.

✔ You want to expose your youngster to roller bladers, bicyclists, skateboarders, and joggers that it might come into contact with while out on walks or near its fenced yard.

✔ You want your Giant to be aware of large vehicles, like garbage trucks, semis, cement mixers, and fire engines, that can pose a threat to the dog that is unaware of them.

✔ Your Giant certainly must be socialized to other dogs and other pets.

✔ Your Giant must be positively introduced to people of different appearances, or different ethnic backgrounds, than you and your family.

Giants, like most other breeds, need to be carefully introduced to things (like a wheelchair in this drawing) that they cannot be expected to understand. By controlling the when and how of the introduction to unusual situations, a Giant owner can also control the dog's response.

✔ Your pup's circle of familiar faces should include repair people, postal workers, and other strangers who must enter your home or yard on occasion.

✔ Your puppy's socialization process should include relatives that visit often.

One of the real tricks of socialization is to keep encounters brief, nonthreatening, and nontraumatizing. Some encounters you set up. For example, if your home has only people of one gender in it, introduce dog-savvy people of the opposite sex with whom your young Giant can play and with whom it can feel comfortable.

Other socialization situations will just happen, like seeing a helicopter or low-flying airplane while out on a walk. Good socialization criteria would give you some good training words that can help settle down a young dog suddenly encountering something unusual. Perhaps a rarely used (in general conversation) control word like *"Whoa"* or *"Steady"* could be introduced as a type of verbal security blanket that will convey to your pet that you are there, that you are in control of the situation, and that everything is fine.

TRAINING AND YOUR GIANT SCHNAUZER

Many people erroneously believe that a pet must be several months old before any training can begin. All canine mothers start training even before the pups have stopped nursing. By utilizing the training techniques that a puppy has already learned from its mother, your job will be quicker, simpler, and more effective.

Training Is Essential

You must begin training your Giant as soon as it comes home. This is essential. You Giant learns its place in your family (its pack) and experiences less confusion and stress. When you take your young Giant to a professional for additional training, you will see many training steps that are patterned after the actions of the pup's first (and many think its best trainer)—its mother. You should follow her methods when training your Giant.

✔ Training and correction should be fair. The canine mother gave each puppy the same lessons and the same treatment. She played no favorites. Her training and her discipline were meted out to each and every puppy in the same manner.

Every dog should be trained, especially a large and powerful Giant Schnauzer.

✔ Correction for misdeeds must be immediate. Puppies have amazingly short attention spans. The mother dealt with any needed discipline within seconds of the act. Your training must also be immediate so that the Giant associates what it did wrong with what you did to correct the wrong.

✔ There is no place for anger in training. A mother dog would never angrily injure a puppy in order to shape its behavior by corrcction. Her behavior modification was done quickly (without long periods of barking at a transgressing pup) and totally without hostility. This is a model that is difficult for some humans to follow, but it is the right way to train a puppy.

✔ Show your Giant love. Love was an integral part of a mother's interaction with her offspring. Her puppies were corrected in a secure, nurturing, and family setting. No pups were thrown out of the whelping box, and no love was withheld from a puppy in error.

✔ Be consistent. The mother was consistent in her actions. Puppies (and especially smart ones like Giant Schnauzers) need consistency in training as with every other element of their lives. An action that got a motherly reprimand one time got the same kind of reprimand the next time. An innocent action that did not call for discipline did not become a misdeed the next time a puppy did the same thing. Puppies learn by repetition followed by positive reinforcement, consistent repetition, and consistent reinforcement.

If you fashion your training after these simple examples of how the mother dog trains, you will become a better trainer. Your pup will then become a better dog.

Training and Pack Behavior

Many aspects of dog ownership trace back to the time when dogs were wild and wolflike. One of the clearest examples of these is the pack concept.

In the wild, life for canines is often brutal and difficult. Enemies abound, and food is usually scarce. Just surviving eludes a high percentage of wild canines. The quest for food burns precious calories for energy that might be needed to escape a large predator.

As with wolves and wild dogs, domestic canines also belong to groups or packs. They are born into their first pack, and their littermates are their fellow pack members. The mother serves as pack leader, and her actions dictate the survival of the pack as a whole. As the puppies mature, they gradually develop their own hierarchy or pecking order within the litter just as wolves and wild canines have in packs.

As mentioned earlier, your Giant Schnauzer puppy will continue to need a pack after it leaves its siblings and mother. You and your family will become your pet's next pack. Each human must become and remain higher on the ladder of dominance than the Giant.

Pack behavior may seem to be some sort of power game when one considers a Giant in submission to all the humans in its home. However, this is a role that dogs not only need but relish. Problems occur when a dog or puppy does not have a clearly defined place. For breeds like the Giant Schnauzer, a lack of pecking order clarity creates a sense of confusion that could lead to serious testing of limits and attempts to climb the family corporate ladder.

One of the main reasons that Giants should not be owned by families with very young children is these childrens' inability to place and maintain a dog in a subservient role. Because it is a Giant characteristic to test and push the boundaries if it can, weaker links in the family pack can end up lower than the dog on the totem pole, something that should *never* be allowed to happen. If family members want the pet to be obedient to them (and they certainly must want this), then all have to be actively involved in the dog's basic training.

Understanding Dog Training

Recalling how the mother dog trained her puppies can provide a glimpse into how the training/learning process occurs. Your Giant

Schnauzer will learn by having the wrong things it does corrected and the right things it does rewarded. This is called positive reinforcement, and it works!

A Giant puppy jumps up into a living room chair and is corrected with a firm *"No!"* Following this authoritative statement, the puppy is very clearly (but gently) lifted out of the chair and onto the floor. The youngster will learn, perhaps after several repetitions, that the chair is off-limits. A problem arises when you do not identically do the same things when the pup jumps up into the chair at a later time. The same problem exists if one member of the family relaxes this rule and allows the puppy to stay in the chair.

Such inconsistency sets up a conflict for the young Giant. When is it right to jump up into the chair, and when is jumping up into the chair wrong? When the puppy is not allowed to stay in the chair, it may feel resentment when reprimanded and removed.

There are many dog-training methodologies in existence from almost Spartan strict to almost laughably lax. The ones that have the best chance of being successful are those (if followed by the entire family) that include the keys to training your Giant Schnauzer just as they were outlined by the actions of the puppy's mother: fair, immediate, without anger, loving, and consistent.

Basic Training

In order for your Giant puppy to begin its life with you, it will need rudimentary or basic training. Teaching your pup the basics should never be considered an end unto itself. The basics merely set the stage for advanced training in the future that may be done by a professional. You can handle the basics. All the members of your Giant Schnauzer's in-home pack must be a part of this training. Their participation will help train the dog and also help them to gain a better understanding of how to train. Basic training thus becomes another item on the commitment list.

Different lines or families of Giants have different aptitudes for training. Some are easier to train, and some are not. The manner in which you chose your puppy now becomes part of the equation. If you chose a pup from the nearest or most convenient breeder or chose a puppy with no recent ancestry that proved to be highly trainable, you may have a problem. If you were careful in your deliberations and found a puppy from a family that had some obedience accomplishments, your task may be much easier. Basic training must include some essentials.

Establish a regular daily training schedule: The best training sessions are not long. Keep them between 10 and 15 minutes in length. Train at times when there are not many distractions. Also, do not schedule training sessions after the pup has been in its crate for a long time. Pent-up energy may make getting down to business difficult.

Training must mean training: As much as you might want to play with your Giant puppy, training times, though they can be fun, are for business and not play. Time to play will come after training has been completed.

Train using the alpha role: In order to gain and keep your pet's attention, you should fill the alpha position with a clear, firm, and authoritarian manner and voice. These alpha aspects are needed to help the pup know that

Positive reinforcement, given in a consistent manner, is the best way to train a Giant Schnauzer.

Training will be much easier if you establish a regular, daily training routine.

training time is different from any other time during the day spent with you and your family.

Training goals must be clear and reachable: Know what you want to accomplish in each session. Be sure your goals are reasonable and then stick to them, doing neither more nor less. The goals have to be clear to the Giant or you are just going through the motions of dog training. Be specific, be clear, and be patient.

Be single-minded: Do not allow your training to meander away from the specific goal of this training session. Stick with what you want your pet to learn today and leave everything else to tomorrow.

Do not double up on your pup: Choose one lesson and do it well rather than two lessons done halfheartedly. No matter how smart your Giant may be, it will do best if each session deals with one topic.

Reward and reinforce: Each time your puppy does what it is supposed to do, give the youngster a reward. Some people train with treats that are given as rewards. Others allow lavish praise to be the reward. Still others use both methods simultaneously.

Remember patience: Remember that your Giant is still a young and inexperienced dog. It wants to please you and will do so if you can convey what you want it to do. Be patient and loving with the puppy.

Training Equipment

You need several pieces of equipment to start training your dog. Two of these are immediate purchases—a training collar and a training lead, or leash. Another, the prong collar, can wait a month or two.

A training collar: Though these fine-link chain collars are commonly called choke collars, this collar, when used correctly, is both humane and effective. You will need another collar for your Giant to hold its dog tags and identification. The training collar is just for training and should be used for nothing else. (Do not leave this collar on the pup when it is not being supervised because the collar could snag on something and frighten or injure the young dog.) When this collar is placed onto your puppy, it should come to realize that playtime is over and training time is at hand. The training collar will allow you to exert some correction and also will not hurt the puppy. The collar should be large enough to go over the widest part of your Giant's head with no more than 1 inch (2.5 cm) of excess length.

A training lead (or leash): When you purchase your training collar (probably at a pet supply store) also buy a 1-inch-wide (2.5-cm-wide) lead, also called a leash. Like the training collar, this training leash will not be used for any other purpose than training. It should be made of leather or woven nylon web material and of very good construction. This training lead should be 6 feet (1.8 m) long. It should have a large (and comfortable) hand loop on one end and a brass or stainless steel swivel snap on the other. This snap will be attached to the ring on your pup's training collar.

Training is essential, because the adult Giant Schnauzer will generally be much stronger than you.

Allow your puppy to become thoroughly familiar and comfortable with both the lead and the collar before you actually begin training with them. It is crucial that your Giant Schnauzer not fear or dislike these important training tools.

The Prong or Pinch Collar

Although far more evil looking than it is, the prong collar is considered by many Giant Schnauzer owners and trainers to be an indispensable piece of gear. This collar resembles a training collar, but it has blunt-pointed prongs turned inward on the collar itself. When properly installed, this collar is very effective against a headstrong dog and quite humane (but controversial, nonetheless). The prong collar pulls down on the dog's neck if it tries to pull away or hang back. The pinch of the prongs is slight but enough to get a pet's attention and keep it on the task at hand.

Before using a prong collar, you should do three things. First, talk with a trainer, handler, or breeder of Giants that has used one extensively.

Then, observe a dog wearing such a collar. Finally, put the collar around your arm (or your own neck) and apply slight pressure to understand the effect it has on the dog.

The Five Basic Commands

You and your family can teach a willing Giant puppy five simple lessons. Prior to training, know that your pet will do better if you keep commands simple. Use a strong alpha voice, and avoid baby talk and other chitchat. Do not string several commands together into a long (and probably incomprehensible) sentence like "Fritz, come over here right now and sit down." Review the list of mother dog training techniques before each session.

Sit

Teaching your Giant pup to sit is a good place to begin its basic training. Your youngster already knows how to sit. It has experienced sitting, and sitting is natural. Now all you really have to do is to teach the dog where, and when, you want it to do what it already knows how to do. The *sit* is also a good first command due to the fact that many other commands begin and/or end in the sitting position.

With the training collar in place around your pet's neck and the training lead attached to the collar, you are prepared for your pup's first lesson. Start with the puppy on your left, next to your left leg. Have only about 12 inches (30 cm) of slack in the lead that you are holding in your right hand.

Firmly, but gently (in a smooth, single, upward motion), lift your pet's head up at the exact same time you gently press downward on the youngster's hindquarters. The upward motion of the head and downward pressure on the pup's hindquarters will force the dog into the sitting position. At the same time, use the dog's name and give the command to sit, "Fritz, *sit.*"

Do not push down with too much force or pull up too sharply. You want the pup to sit down, not to feel hurt or get into a contest of wills with you. As soon as the puppy sits, give it lots of praise (or perhaps a small treat if that is your approach to rewards). You want the puppy to have a happy association of reward when it does what the command told it to do.

Repeat this process several times in your first training sessions. Take your time. The *sit* is important, and the puppy must know it thoroughly before you move on to the next basic command. A smart pup like your Giant should have little trouble mastering the *sit.* Soon the young dog will be sitting without any pressure on its hindquarters at all. After the puppy has clearly learned this command, each of the other members of your family should go through a sit session or two with the puppy, doing exactly what you have already done. This will associate in your pup's mind this command with all the humans in your home while teaching them the right way to use the command.

Stay

Following the *sit* is the *stay.* The *stay* actually starts in the *sit* position with the pup in position next to your left leg. Once again, the lead is in your right hand and is used to hold the pup's head up. In a clear, alpha voice, give the command (with the dog's name) "Fritz, *stay"* as you step straight forward, away from the sitting puppy, leading with your right foot. As you give the command and step out, bring

***The* stay *command generally makes use of the palm of the trainer's hand with the voice command* "Stay."**

the palm of your left hand down in front of the pup's face as if you were trying to do an upside-down version of the familiar traffic cop's hand signal for stop.

The *stay* has four distinct parts that must be done at the same time:

1. You gently use pressure to keep the pup's head up;

2. You step forward, leading with your right foot;

3. Your left hand is in a stop or blocking motion in front of the pup's face; and

4. You use your alpha voice to say, "Fritz (or whatever your dog's name is), *stay.*"

The *stay* may be hard for some puppies. It is a conflicting command. It makes a puppy that wants to be with you see you step away and leave it behind.

Repeat this lesson several times, but do not tire the young Giant. If the pup has difficulty with this command, do not push it to learn the *stay* completely in one session (or several sessions). Always end on a positive note with the command that the pup has accomplished, the *sit.* Do a couple of *sits,* and reward the pup for doing them before you end each lesson.

The *stay* is one of the tougher basic commands. However, most dogs can do it, and it can be accomplished by your Giant Schnauzer. Use patience in teaching this command. Do the command in the same way each time, omitting no steps. Soon, longer for some pups than others, your Giant will be staying for short periods. Praise should be given for any length of *stay.* Over time, these *stay* periods will last longer and longer. After the young dog has the *stay* in control, do the same thing with this command that you did with the *sit.* Bring your family in to put the dog through the *stay* (they must do it just like you do, even using the authoritative voice). The *stay* command has a release word that lets the dog know that it can stop staying and join you. Saying *"OK"* will let the puppy know that it can come to be with you and be rewarded for its good behavior.

Heel

The *heel* command is very necessary if you want to go anywhere with your pet. *Heel* is also very important with Giant Schnauzers that may want to test their strength against whoever is holding the leash. A poorly trained dog can not only be a nuisance to walk but could bolt into a busy street with a lighter person on the other end of the leash. (See "The Prong or Pinch Collar" on page 57 for older puppies that have a desire to test dominance by pulling.)

A puppy's mother will already have begun the training process. Try to follow her training style: firm, consistent, appropriate, and loving.

A black Giant with uncropped ears and an undocked tail participates in a Schutzhund trial in Germany.

The **heel** *command begins with the puppy beside the trainer's left foot and with the training leash held in the trainer's right hand, guided by the left hand.*

Like the *stay,* the *heel* command starts off in the *sit* position. (Both the *sit* and the *stay* must be mastered before attempting to teach the *heel.*) The lead is in your right hand. The young Giant is sitting beside your left foot. While using your alpha voice, you say, "Fritz, *heel."* Step off, leading with your left foot for this command. If the pup does not move with you, pop the slack portion of the lead (in your right hand) against the side of your leg (to get the dog's attention) and keep walking. Not having the palm of your left hand blocking its view should encourage the Giant to step out with you. Continue the gentle pressure to keep the pup's head up and moving with you. As the pup gets the hang of it and starts to walk by your left side, give it praise, but do not stop walking. Keep moving and keep praising as long as the young Giant stays right by your side. If your pup has trouble with the *heel* command, do not exert

Training involves conveying what you want a dog to do in a way the dog can understand it.

When a Giant Schnauzer is well socialized and properly trained, it is a joy to its family, a credit to the breed, and a truly happy animal.

force to drag the youngster along beside you. Go back to the *sit* command, and start over again. The *heel* allows the pup to be with you, which is something a Giant Schnauzer always wants to do. So the *heel* needs only a little patience and consistency before your pet knows how to do it.

Unlike the other commands with which you want to involve your family as cotrainers, wait until the puppy is really good at obediently doing the *heel* before letting a smaller person try this command. The prong collar might be of use when your family tries the *heel* command.

The *heel* is a very useful everyday command. You can continue the training process while you are walking with your pet and when you are out on socialization visits. Patience and consistency will help your youngster learn how to walk with you and not lag behind, surge ahead, or take side trips.

Down

The *down* command utilizes elements of both the *sit* and the *stay*. The *down* calls for your pet to drop down onto its stomach from a *sit*

The* come *command is easily taught, but it can be untaught by calling your pet to come to you for some unpleasant reason (bathing, correction, and so forth).* Never *call your pet to you when it will experience something unpleasant if it obeys the command.* Always *go to the pet on these occasions.

position and then remain there. While the leash remains in your right hand, instead of exerting upward pressure to keep the pup's head up, the *down* requires downward pressure to pull the head (and the stomach) downward.

As you pull downward on the lead (some trainers actually run the lead under their shoe to get a straight *down* movement), you give the command, "Fritz, *down.*" As you pull downward with your right hand and give the verbal command, make a bouncing-ball motion with your left hand right in front of the Giant's face. These elements of the *down* should be done at the same time to convey to the pup that it is to drop down onto its stomach. The spoken command reinforces the physical pull, and the hand signal also gives the dog some idea of what you want. This command must be begun while you still have physical superiority over your Giant Schnauzer.

Because the command also has a *stay* component, you must start praising even as the puppy's stomach touches the floor or the ground. This praise and the gradual learning of the *stay* will help the pup learn how to do the *down* without much difficulty. Training the Giant youngster to stay in the *down* will call for patience, positive reinforcement, and

TIP

Do Not Stop with the Basics

Several places in this book have pointed out that Giant Schnauzers can be better pets with advanced training. While you and your family may have done an excellent job training your pet for the basic commands, there are still many things that you cannot teach your pet. This advanced training is best done using real professionals.

Your veterinarian, breed mentor, or some of your contacts with the world of Giant Schnauzers can help guide you to experienced trainers who have ample experience with dogs like yours. As you did when you sought your puppy, seek the best available trainer (preferably one that has experience with and a liking for Giants), pay the cost of advanced training, and expect your pet to be the better for it.

One of the best things you can do for your Giant puppy (and for yourself) is to enroll the puppy in a training class. Not only do you and your puppy learn from expert trainers, but being around other puppies and people helps with socialization.

consistency. This is also a command that your family may be able to assist with after the young dog has thoroughly mastered it.

Come

At first glance, this seems like a simple command. In some aspects, it is. In other ways, the *come* command has some tricky parts that can make it harder to teach and harder to learn. Some things about the *come* command that make it unique include the following.

✔ Your alpha voice must exude more cheerfulness and fun than the command sounds of the other commands.

✔ Your physical role is different as you have to be inviting, dropping to one knee and spreading your arms open wide to encourage your pet to run quickly to you.

✔ You can overdo the *come* command and make it seem like just another word to a dog. Use the word when you want the actual presence of the dog at your side, then reward the dog for doing what you want.

✔ You can untrain the command by incorrectly saying it. Never call your pet to you for some negative thing, and do not allow the members of your family to do so. If a pup gets something it perceives as bad when it obeys the *come* command, it will not obey that command for long.

✔ One way to teach a puppy to come is to use a long cotton lead to pull the pup to you slowly as you give the command.

✔ Never underestimate the importance of this command when a Giant Schnauzer is involved. A dog that will not come is not a fully trained dog. It could be a candidate for a quick death under the wheels of a car or because of a fight with another dog.

✔ Help your pet stay safe and obedient by teaching and then using the *come* command correctly.

FEEDING YOUR GIANT SCHNAUZER

Without good nutrition, no Giant Schnauzer will ever be able to meet its complete genetic potential (mentally or physically). As with human children, the lack of food containing the needed vitamins and minerals will affect a Giant in the most negative manner.

Although a Giant Schnauzer is not truly a giant breed, being as much as 10 inches (25 cm) shorter than some tall Great Danes or Irish Wolfhounds and 75 pounds (35 kg) lighter than some Mastiffs and Saint Bernards, the breed is still quite large and fast growing. Rapid growth can often cause real health problems. An appropriate diet is essential to the Giant as it grows up, as it matures as an active dog, and as it reaches its senior years.

Special Feeding Considerations

In every breed, there are levels of breeder involvement. Creative breeders have developed special approaches to very nearly every aspect of ownership, care, and development of Giants. While every responsible breeder (and many responsible dog owners) would never suggest table scraps or even human meals for their pets, some breeders have developed their own diets for Giants.

Sleek coat, firm muscles, and overall health can all be traced back to a carefully balanced diet.

A word of caution to the novice Giant Schnauzer owner is in order here. If you are going to follow the dietary/nutritional plans of some respected breeder, follow it completely and to the very letter. Where some beginners get into trouble (and one of the reasons the author recommends using super-premium dry foods) is that they lack the commitment to the exactness of the top-breeder diets. One cannot follow such diets half the time, or three-quarters of the time, or even 90 percent of the time. Special diets are to be followed devotedly, without substitution, without variation, and without inconsistency of any sort.

These diets may vary in minor points among the breeders that advocate them, but none of the feeding plans developed by widely acknowledged breed experts is the product of chance. Dog breeders at this level are very serious about their Giant Schnauzers. They want nothing but the best dogs, nothing but the best from their dogs, and nothing but the best for their dogs.

Most breeder-developed special diets involve actual meat and other foods carefully measured and blended for quality of ingredients, palatability, and nutritional content. Some breeders may prefer different ingredients within their mixtures. However, most of these Giant expert feeding plans have a great degree of similarity between one another.

The Importance of Nutritional Balance

Whether a dog's food is a top-quality superpremium commercial food or a top-quality breeder version, every successful diet must be balanced. If a pet's food lacks balance in any area, your Giant Schnauzer will not become what it has the genetic heritage to be.

Balance in a dog or puppy food simply means that the diet will have, in the correct percentages, the key elements of proteins, carbohydrates, fats, vitamins, and minerals. Although these building blocks must be in every canine diet, the proportions of each in a specific dog's diet may differ due to the age and activity level of that dog.

Despite the growth and variation in pet foods, the basic tenets of balance must be observed. Without the essential underpinning of proteins, carbohydrates, fats, vitamins, and minerals, no food (no matter how exotic its ingredients or how expansive its advertising) can provide all that a Giant will need to develop fully both physically and mentally.

The Elements of a Good Nutritional Plan

Each bag or can of commercial pet food is required to have a guaranteed analysis of what is in that food (in very general terms) printed on the packaging. Depending on the age of your Giant and its activity level, a food will have different percentages of proteins, carbohydrates, and fats. The guaranteed analysis will also show the percentages of moisture and fiber in the food.

With the help of your Giant's breeder, your breed mentor, and your veterinarian, you will come to understand the percentages of key elements thought best for the ages and needs of different individual pets. While opinions will vary about brands, ingredients, and product claims, the guaranteed analysis will give you a broad and general picture of the balance of the food.

Water

You will not see drinking water listed on the guaranteed analysis on the packaging of commercial pet foods, but water is of crucial importance. Lots of pure, fresh water available to your Giant at all times is as important an aspect of nutritional balance as any other. Active dogs like the Giants will need large amounts of water, especially if they are fed dry dog foods, which are low in moisture content.

Commercial Pet Foods

Your dog's breeder, your breed mentor, and others within the circle of Giant Schnauzer

There are many good pet foods on the market, but follow the advice of your dog's breeder, your breed mentor, and your veterinarian. Above all, find a good food and stay with it.

people that you have come to know can help you find a commercial food that will meet the needs of your dog. Listen to those who have been involved with Giants for a number of years and who have staked the success of their own dogs on the foods they are recommending. Follow their suggestions as to amounts, frequency, and specifics because different families of Giants may tend to do better on one food than on another. Remember the watchword of *consistency* in feeding (as in so many other areas of Giant ownership).

Do not fall into a trap of bad habits by shifting your pet from food to food to food. Find Giant Schnauzer experts on whom you can depend, and listen carefully to which commercial brands they recommend. Your Giant will do better on a consistent diet fed in a consistent manner.

Canned dog foods (sometimes referred to as wet dog foods) have been widely accepted. Though popular, canned foods come with a set of both positive and negative aspects. Positive aspects of caned foods include the following:

✔ They are extremely palatable, and dogs tend to eat them readily.

✔ Canned foods are generally quite meaty looking and have a variety of aromas.

✔ They have long shelf life, are easy to store, and are vermin proof.

✔ Canned foods are convenient to use, requiring only a can opener and no heavy lifting or bags to open.

✔ Canned foods do work well as mixers with dry food.

✔ They are easy to feed in one-meal sizes.

Canned foods are not without their negatives.

✔ They are the most expensive form of pet food, a factor to consider with a large dog like the Giant Schnauzer.

✔ Canned foods are between 75 and 85 percent moisture; once opened, they spoil quickly if not immediately eaten.

✔ Diets exclusively of canned foods tend to cause or contribute to more tartar and other dental problems in dogs.

✔ Canned or wet foods promote smelly, messy, and loose stools.

Dry dog foods are the most popular form of food fed by most owners of large breeds. As with canned foods, there are minuses and pluses involved with their use. Some of the positive aspects of feeding dry foods include the following.

✔ They are generally the most cost-effective, especially in the larger bags.

✔ Quality dry foods have the highest digestibility, with stool firmness and decreased stool size (both good measures of food efficiency in dogs) best with these diets.

✔ Although no food or treat is a substitute for regular dental attention and care, dry foods aid in reducing film and tartar buildup.

✔ The best dry foods can be fed from whelping box to the grave because they are designed to be complete diets for dogs at varying ages.

✔ Short-term storage is good with dry forms of dog foods.

An excellent coat on a Giant will depend on the excellence of the proteins and fats in its food.

✔ When fed correctly, the dry-food diets are not as likely to lead to obesity as are canned versions.

Note, however, that dry foods do have negative aspects.

✔ Dry foods have very low moisture content and require lots of fresh water to be readily available for your Giant.

✔ In some climates (and under some conditions), dry foods in paper bags may have long-term storage problems from bag breakage, heat spoilage, external water damage, and vermin.

✔ The quality of dry foods varies greatly, ranging from grocery store brands to the superpremiums, which can be confusing to beginning dog owners.

Any Giant Schnauzer engaged in heavy physical activities, whether being shown or being bred, will require a high-quality premium dog food.

Other types of dog food: Although dry and canned foods are the most popular types, other forms of pet nutrition are available. One of these is the semimoist foods. These rather expensive, often dye-laden foods are generally tasty to dogs. They come in shapes that look like hamburgers, meatballs, and small cuts of meat. They are most often seen in grocery stores and are rarely used in any large amounts by serious breeders of large dogs. They are useful on trips or as treats, being in convenient foil packaging. However, they do have some spoilage concerns.

Feeding a Giant Puppy

The first rule in feeding a puppy is not to change what it has been fed by its original owners. Since you have gone to the best-possible source for your young Giant (this excludes most backyard breeders, puppy mills, pet automats, and flea markets), you have come into contact with someone who has chosen wisely what he or she feeds puppies.

Your new Giant Schnauzer will already be going through a great deal of trauma and stress at being uprooted from its mother and littermates. Do not add to this emotional discomfort by piling dietary change on top of everything else. Feed what your breeder has been feeding (even if it runs counter to what some of your other advisors may be telling you). The time to change a pet's food is not in the first months of its life.

If you absolutely must change, then make the shift from one food to another as slowly and gradually as possible. Regardless of what some information from pet food makers and other pet professionals may say, one week is not enough time to change puppy foods gradually.

Consistency is important in all aspects of puppy feeding, probably even more important than it is for an adult dog and an older dog. A puppy will need to be fed about four times each day. Feed the same amount each time, and accustom the youngsters to eating at the same times each day. Regular amounts of food fed at regular times will also help a puppy become more regular in its bowel habits.

Just as dog food isn't designed for the nutritional needs of humans, so human food isn't the best choice for dogs. Another benefit of not feeding table scraps is that you are allowed to eat your dinner without your Giant begging for food from your plate.

A litter should be closely monitored as it grows to see which puppies are thriving on their diet and which may need extra help from the breeder.

As a puppy grows up, the number of feedings can be decreased to three and then (as it nears maturity) to two meals per day. *Gradual* and *consistent* are the key words here. Abrupt changes are not good for a dog and especially for a baby dog.

Remember that a Giant will become only the pet that its environment allows it to become. This is certainly true of diet. Size, disposition, mental acuity, coat and skin, musculature, bone structure, and overall health are all affected by what a pet eats. This is especially so when that pet is a fast-growing, high-energy Giant Schnauzer puppy.

Feeding the large-breed puppy diets can greatly aid a Giant puppy. These foods have been specially formulated for the specific needs of youngsters that have a lot of growing to do in a relatively short time. Some Giant breeders recommend that quality large-breed puppy foods be fed to young Giants for as long as two years.

Feeding a Giant Adult

Many dog owners make a common mistake. They have an older puppy that looks very much like an adult dog. They have been conscientiously feeding a quality puppy food and need to buy some more. At the pet supply store, they suddenly decide it is time for Fritz to be switched to adult food. They impulsively purchase the adult food (of the same brand as their puppy food) instead of the puppy food they were seeking.

Just because the same company makes a food does not mean that it can be immediately

Feeding routines for very large dogs can vary from common practices with smaller animals. Some breeders recommend keeping a Giant on high-quality large-breed puppy food up to its second birthday.

An effective feeding routine often depends on a dog's activity level. Therefore, the diet of a relative "couch potato" can vary considerably from a Giant Schnauzer that competes in dog shows or performance events or is used in any type of high-stress work.

replaced by another food made by the same company. Regardless of what company literature or representatives may say, such a change should be handled just as if one were shifting to an entirely new brand.

Your veterinarian, your breed mentor, and your dog's breeder should be consulted before you move your Giant Schnauzer from puppy food to adult food. There is no universal, magical date or age at which you must change foods. Much depends on the line or family of your Giant. Some lines mature earlier than others do. Your breed experts and your veterinarian can help you assess when the time is right for such a dietary change for your pet. Some Giant breeders do not feed their pups puppy foods very long to avoid young dogs growing too fast and putting too much weight onto a skeleton not yet fully developed. Others take the more traditional approach that leads a pup from mother's milk to puppy food to adult food to senior food.

Adult dogs will normally not need the same amounts of proteins and fats that a rapidly growing puppy will need. Adults also do not need the same number of feedings per day that young pups do. Dog foods that have been developed for the needs of large-breed adults fit well into this picture of maintaining mature health rather than building juvenile bone and muscle. Such foods have been a godsend to experts and beginners alike who want to keep their Giant Schnauzers in good condition.

Normally, your adult Giant will do well on a quality adult diet (whether commercial or by one of the top breeders). If your adult Giant is involved in Schutzhund, dog shows, breeding, or other activities that can require more nutrition, adult foods for performance dogs can be used in lieu of regular adult food.

It is important to make your dog's food fit the needs of the adult dog and not the other way around. The right food will allow the dog to be very active (as Giants are) without promoting overfeeding, which could lead to weight problems. Giants are not meant to look like large fuzzy sausages like some Miniature Schnauzers. The right food in the right amounts will do wonders in keeping your pet in good health.

One of the most important elements in any dog's diet is clean, fresh water—and lots of it!

Feeding the Older Giant

As dogs get older, their nutritional needs change. Unlike so many of the larger dogs, Giant Schnauzers tend to be fairly long-lived. A Giant Schnauzer at seven is still in its prime, while a Great Dane or Mastiff is already considered an old dog at the same age. Because the aging process is not as rapid in Giant Schnauzers, a time will come when the older dog will no longer need performance food because it has retired from the strenuous activities that required such a diet. A time will also come when the adult food that a Giant has been eating is no longer what the dog needs.

Fortunately, the top makers of pet foods have developed senior diets that help hold the oldster in good shape without promoting weight problems. Some companies have taken this even a step further and have designed foods for larger breed older dogs that take in the added need for bone and joint strength in larger oldsters.

Even with foods designed for the unique needs of larger dogs, you must again carefully shift a senior Giant from an adult ration onto a more appropriate diet for its age and physical requirements. Special size-specific foods have taken some of the guesswork about how to provide for your dog adequately as it grows up and then grows older.

Senior foods have even less fat and protein levels than do adult foods. Older dogs do not need the energy-making fats, and they have grown all they are going to grow. If a senior dog has a lot of fat in its diet and this fat is not burned up by physical activity, the fat must go somewhere. It then tends to build up on the dog.

Your veterinarian can be a great help to you in knowing when to switch an active adult onto a senior food designed for decreased activity. Your breed mentor and your dog's breeder may also be able to share what they have seen in feeding other senior Giant Schnauzers, some even close relatives of your dog.

Feeding the Spayed or Neutered Giant

One of the fallacies about spaying or neutering a pet is that surgically stopping a pet's ability to reproduce will inevitably make the animal become fat. While it is possible for such pets to gain weight and become obese, some overweight dogs have not been spayed or neutered. If a spayed female or neutered male is given ample exercise, feeding it should be no different than for most other Giants of the same age and activity level.

Some Giants are more prone to gaining weight than others, whether they are intact breeders or not. Many excellent commercial dog foods are labeled as light or reduced-calorie diets. These products are readily available and can be a good way, along with a lack of table scraps and lots of exercise, to keep a Giant in shape.

YOUR GIANT SCHNAUZER'S HEALTH

Part of the commitment of being a Giant owner is dealing with health matters for your pet. Even a large and vigorous breed can face sickness or injury from time to time. To minimize ailments and hurts and to maximize good health, you need to prevent and treat health problems. Each of these is part of the Giant commitment process. Each of these will require some intelligent planning on the part of you and your family. Each will be only as effective as the timely fashion in which it has been undertaken.

Prevention—Important Tips

Prevention of sickness and injuries is a multifaceted approach. It calls on you to be aware, available, and anticipatory in dealing with those diseases and those accidental injuries that can be stopped before they stop your Giant. Many of these have been discussed in detail in this text.

You have already begun preventing health problems by carefully searching for a Giant puppy from healthy sources and parentage. Perhaps as much as any other single factor, your research and wise selecting will set the stage for a long and healthy life for your Giant.

A healthy Giant Schnauzer exudes vigor and vitality.

Another way that you have already begun the prevention process is by effectively puppy proofing your pet's environment. This means removing dangers and hurtful situations before bringing a puppy into your home, yard, car, and other puppy-accessible places.

You have also made a major stride toward preventing health problems by seeking out a good veterinarian in your community and by enlisting that medical professional's invaluable help in assessing the needs and preventive measures for your Giant. This includes being certain that your pet gets all its immunizations, boosters, and other medications as needed.

Parasite control and hygiene are significant. Not only do fleas make a dog miserable, they may also cause a severe allergic reaction.

Start your new Giant off right with an immediate visit to your veterinarian. If you follow this practice throughout the dog's life, that life will be healthier and longer.

Not only are ticks repulsive, but they can harbor serious diseases that can affect pets and humans.

Spaying and neutering your Giant is crucial to its health. Not only will such surgery prevent certain illnesses, but it will also eliminate some biological drives that can put a good Giant into a dangerous spot.

Follow your breeder's, breed mentor's, and veterinarian's advice. Do not take a not fully immunized, vulnerable puppy to places where it can come into contact with and/or possibly contract serious, potentially fatal diseases.

Training is another preventive aspect that directly affects the health of a Giant. The thoroughly trained dog has a much better chance at stopping at the edge of a business highway when commanded to do so than a poorly trained (or completely untrained) dog.

Socialization is another preventive focus. The Giant that has been thoroughly and correctly socialized is much less of a liability to other animals, other people, and itself. A poorly socialized pet can bite someone. Often, a death sentence is imposed by governmental authorities on biting ("vicious") dogs.

Quality nutrition in a well-designed feeding plan carried out in an appropriate and consistent manner can add years to a Giant's life. Simultaneously, strong and high fences, good collars and leads, and crate training are control elements that will help keep a Giant from harmful situations and impromptu excursions that could lead to serious injury or death.

You and your family's absolute refusal to let the Giant become the dominant force in your family will inevitably save its life. Many dogs (some of them Giant Schnauzers) have been given up by their families to uncertain lives and possible death at an animal shelter when they have proven themselves to be uncontrollable and insistent on being boss.

Common sense can deflect danger from your dog. Using carriers or canine seat belts when traveling by car, avoiding leaving dogs in hot vehicles, and keeping pets away from poison are but three of a long list of things a proactive and thinking pet owner can do.

Having a safety-conscious and health-conscious mentality means you and your family will take this list and personalize it to your own situation and lifestyle. The important thing is to establish this kind of mentality as a high priority for you and your family. Doing so may save your Giant's life.

Treatment

When disease strikes or injury occurs, a committed Schnauzer-owning family will have a treatment plan worked out well in advance. This plan will help shorten the time the pet is affected by the disease and also decrease the severity of the injury. It will also curb complications of both.

While actual treatment should ordinarily be done under a trained veterinarian's care, many things can be done to enhance a course of treatment action. Some of these include the following.

✔ Establish a clear and ongoing rapport with your Giant's veterinarian, demonstrating your (and your family's) level of commitment to the dog. Follow your veterinarian's suggestions and home treatment plan explicitly, carefully, and conscientiously.

✔ Take your Giant to the clinic when it is supposed to be there for regular checkups and follow-up visits. In the event of serious disease or accident, call to alert the veterinarian and move expeditiously to get your Giant under the practitioner's care as soon as possible.

✔ Do not try to heal your pet with home remedies or with quackery. Your veterinarian is trained in the healing of pets; let the professional do the job.

✔ Study ailments and possible genetic conditions that may specifically affect your Giant. Among these are CHD (canine hip dysplasia) and gastric torsion or bloat.

Immunizations

The world of a Giant Schnauzer can be filled with a large number of serious diseases, some of which could prove fatal to an unprotected animal. Fortunately for dogs in general, and your Giant specifically, veterinary science has provided a number of vaccinations that can prevent the onset of the most serious of these diseases.

Vaccinations for rabies, distemper, hepatitis, leptospirosis, parvovirus (and coronavirus), and parainfluenza (and bordetella) are usually given one at a time or in groups when a puppy is between the ages of one to six months of life. Full immunization against these fatal diseases requires that a Giant youngster receive the entire series of shots. A first round of vaccinations may have been given while your pup was still with its breeder. Your veterinarian can help you schedule appropriate times for the remaining immunizations. Annual boosters are needed so adult dogs can keep these diseases at bay.

Rabies: The vaccination for rabies is generally given after some of the other immunizations. Though now relatively rare in domestic animals in the United States (in comparison to early, preimmunization times), rabies is still present in many wild, warm-blooded mammals. Many municipalities mandate that all pets have rabies vaccinations (administered by licensed and approved veterinarians) when pups are three months old.

Rabies can turn a wonderful and loving family pet into a death-dealing mad dog. Imagine the nightmare that an unimmunized adult Giant Schnauzer could be in a neighborhood. Not only could such a dog infect other animals with this incurable, viral disease, but rabies (through a bite or saliva into an open wound)

Young Giants need regular immunizations and good veterinary care to reach their physical and genetic potential.

is transmittable to humans. As a pet owner, you are not only responsible for adequate immunization against rabies for your Giant puppy but for continued reimmunization for your adult dog as well. Laws regarding the frequency of the ongoing rabies vaccinations vary from community to community. Your veterinarian can help you comply with this good-sense and good-health law.

Canine distemper (CD): Historically, distemper has been one of the greatest killers of dogs and other canines. In past centuries, entire kennels and even some breeds have been wiped out by canine distemper. Even with the highly effective vaccines of the new millennium, CD continues to pose a potent threat to young puppies. Because it is spread primarily by body secretions (urine, feces, and nasal mucus), distemper is highly contagious and can be spread by contact with clothing, equipment, and other dog paraphernalia that has come into contact with the secretions of an infected animal. Although unimmunized animals of any age can be affected by distemper, it is especially fatal to puppies.

The symptoms of this neurological disease can include mild "colds" with slight fevers, coughing, discharges from the nose and the eyes, poor or nonexistent appetite, seizures and convulsions, lack of coordination, involuntary muscle spasms, and diarrhea. CD can kill unvaccinated young pups almost overnight, or it can affect them for several days only to die later. On rare occasions puppies do not die from canine distemper, but they are generally never healthy for the rest of their lives.

The first in several vaccinations for CD are given to puppies at six weeks of age. This immunization comes in a series, often combined with other preventatives. Yearly boosters are required to keep your Giant Schnauzer safe from this ancient (and current) killer.

Canine adenovirus, type 1 (CAV-1), commonly called hepatitis or infectious canine hepatitis, is not the same disease that affects human beings. CAV-1 is a highly contagious, fatal illness with no known cure. This systematic liver-damaging ailment that can cause rapid death in vulnerable puppies may even look somewhat like CD.

CAV-1 can be spread to a puppy through the air (from bodily secretions of infected animals) or through tainted food or water. A puppy with infectious canine hepatitis may have a high fever, abdominal tenderness, bloody diarrhea, and vomiting.

Fortunately, CAV-1 is effectively controlled by vaccinations (often given in combined form

Activities like Schutzhund training (which emphasizes obedience and control, not attack aggression) require that a Giant be in the best possible physical condition.

with other vaccines). These begin at about six weeks of age and include annual booster shots.

Leptospirosis: Another deadly illness spread by contact with urine from a sick animal is leptospirosis, which attacks a puppy's kidneys. Even when effective treatment of this disease saves a puppy's life, permanent kidney damage is a likely result. Humans and animals other than canines can also contract leptospirosis.

Initially, it causes vomiting, excessive thirst, muscle pain, increased urination, and jaundice. Leptospirosis is caused by a spiral-shaped bacteria called a spirochete. Dogs that have had this disease may infect other animals for several years. Usually combined with vaccines for CD and CAV, the immunization for leptospirosis is generally given at or before six weeks of age.

Parvovirus: Young puppies are particularly susceptible to parvovirus. This primarily attacks a young dog's immune system, bone marrow, gastrointestinal tract, and heart, although it can strike at any age. Some breeds are especially vulnerable to parvovirus, among them the close relative of the Giant Schnauzer—the Doberman.

While severity varies in parvovirus, young dogs with this disease suffer from severe dehydration stemming from heavy bouts with diarrhea and vomiting. Parvo (as it is commonly called) can kill an affected dog or puppy within two days, but immediate veterinary care can save some victims.

Some veterinarians administer parvovirus vaccine four times, starting at six weeks of age and continuing every three weeks until the puppy reaches 18 weeks of age. Additionally, this vaccine may also be incorporated with a final immunization cocktail for CD, CAV-1, and leptospirosis. Follow the guidelines that your Giant Schnauzer's veterinarian will recommend about this and all immunizations.

Canine coronavirus infection: Like parvo, coronavirus can vary in severity. Both dogs and puppies can become infected with this highly contagious disease. While most outbreaks in adults are minor, puppies can be severely weakened by coronavirus and become prey for other killers like parvovirus.

One special characteristic of coronavirus is the resultant diarrhea that the disease brings. Loose, foul-smelling stools, orange in color and tinged with blood and mucus, are apparent coronavirus indicators.

Immunizations for coronavirus are usually given with others at six weeks. Annual boosters are part of the preventative regimen. While this viral infection can be treated, keeping it away from your Giant Schnauzer is the far more preferable course of action.

Bordetella (kennel cough): Although scientifically labeled *Bordetella bronchiseptica*, this highly contagious but relatively mild disease is often a fellow traveler of tracheobronchitis. Bordetella can complicate treatment for this other ailment. An immunization (followed by annual or biannual boosters) can usually prevent or lessen the severity of this respiratory illness marked by severe recurrent episodes of coughing.

Dogs with bordetella spread the disease, as carriers, to others in their kennels with whom they come into contact. Recovered dogs can continue to spread the disease for up to three months. Good kennel hygiene and quarantining affected animals may help keep Giant Schnauzer puppies from being needlessly subjected to this infection.

Parasites

As if dread diseases and various kinds of medical conditions were not enough to threaten your Giant Schnauzer, a large number of parasites plague animals. Although most of these are not life threatening, they can pull down the physical condition of your Giant and introduce potentially fatal diseases into its system. Some parasites live inside your pet (some are inherited from its mother) and some live outside. Some of these are minor irritations, but others can cause major health problems for a pet.

Internal Parasites

Intestinal parasites can severely affect the vigor and overall health of your Giant Schnauzer puppy. This is especially so of roundworms, whipworms, and hookworms. These parasites can be handled effectively by regular visits to your veterinarian. Home remedies for worms and over-the-counter treatments are risky for your Giant puppy. Let your veterinarian deal with these pests.

Roundworms are among the most common of internal parasites to inflict themselves onto pet animals. Roundworm larvae may remain unseen and dormant in a mother dog's body (perhaps for her entire life) and then insert themselves into fetal puppies in her womb. Dogs can also become infested with round-

Your Giant should be immunized early, and these immunizations should always be kept current.

worms through ingestion of worm eggs from the soil, feces, or similar sources.

Humans, especially children, may also have infestations of roundworms. A cycle of roundworms in the pet that then go back into the ground only to come back to the pet amply explains the widespread nature of theses pests.

Giant Schnauzer puppies with roundworms may fail to develop to their full potential. They may be stunted, have dull coats, and take on the classical roundworm look of a greatly distended abdomen, which the unknowing think of as cute. Other illnesses, like pneumonia, can attack a weakened puppy's defenses and turn a parasite into a direct cause of death.

Whipworms: Dogs of all ages can have whipworms. These worms are usually found in the colon and cecum of puppies and dogs. They are generally hidden in view and effect but can cause severe diarrhea, chronically and intermittently. Kennels have to be treated to keep whipworms from reinfesting pets time after time. Whipworms are tough customers that resist all but the most diligent efforts to clear them from a pet's environment.

Hookworms, like roundworms, can be found in dogs of all ages. These bloodsuckers are especially hard on puppies and cause a lack of vigor and vitality in infested youngsters. Your Giant will not become the pet or adult that it could become if it is weighed down physically by hookworms.

One indicator of hookworms is blood in puppy stools, which can also appear very tar-like and nearly black in color. A Giant Schnauzer puppy with hookworms will show signs of loss of blood—pale gums, emaciation, weakness, anemia, and a reduced ability to fight off disease. Some puppies may require blood transfusions to survive the onslaught of hookworms.

Hookworms are spread through skin contact or through ingestion of worm eggs. Some mother dogs can pass this pest on to their offspring in utero or shortly after birth.

Tapeworms hitchhike into your pet's body through another parasite—the flea. Fleas (and lice) play host to the tapeworm. Fleas bite your Giant and can pass along tapeworms to your pet. Long, flat, and segmented, tapeworms do minor damage to most dogs, but they do sap some of your pet's energy and condition.

To get rid of tapeworms requires a strict endeavor to get rid of their carriers, fleas, and lice. Keep fleas and lice away from your Giant, and you will also prevent infestation from tapeworms.

Heartworms: Like the tapeworm, the heartworm is another parasite that comes to your Giant courtesy of another pest. Heartworms are transmitted to pets (and wild animals also) through the bite of a mosquito that is carrying heartworm larvae. The mosquito bites your pet and inserts some fluid into the dog to encourage blood flow. This fluid also deposits heartworm larvae into your dog.

These larvae enter the dog's bloodstream and gravitate toward the animal's heart, where they will grow and eventually clog the heart. This clogging is fatal and will continue until the affected animal dies.

Once thought to be only a problem of the southern United States, heartworms have now spread to many other areas of the United States and other countries. The diagnosis for heartworms is made using a blood test. An owner-administered pill given monthly can easily prevent heartworms. This medication must be prescribed by a veterinarian and should follow a test to determine if prevention or treatment is needed.

Even simple walks and romps in the backyard or park expose your Giant to diseases, parasites, and other health problems.

External Parasites

Fleas and ticks are the most common external parasites that pester dogs. They are the bane of many a dog's existence as they literally feast on the blood of their host—the dog.

Fleas: When fleas are present in great numbers, they can cause some pets to become anemic. Anemia can be fatal, especially to very young dogs and very old dogs.

Some dogs, like some people, have severe allergic reactions to fleabites. Dogs with this allergic reaction scratch incessantly. Hair loss results from the dog's attempt to rid itself of the fleas. Fleas cause much more misery for many dogs than do almost any other parasite, external or internal.

To keep your Giant Schnauzer free of fleas, you may have to learn something from the dog itself. Just as your Giant guards you, you must be alert and on guard to keep fleas out of your pet's hair and environment. The Giant Schnauzer is a no-nonsense dog that is very serious about its territory and family. A serious approach must be taken regarding fleas. Some approaches to deal with fleas include the following.

✔ Ask your veterinarian to prescribe something to keep fleas away from your dog, perhaps one of the flea spot products or the flea deterrent pill.

✔ Keep your pet clean and away from places where fleas might choose to relocate from tall grass or bushy undergrowth.
✔ In consultation with your veterinarian, use shampoos, sprays, and flea collars where appropriate. (Always remember to check whether some current flea remedy might be contraindicated with the remedies you are already using.)
✔ Remember that fleas spend the vast majority (90 percent) of their lives off the dog. This means that the fleas are somewhere in your environment—lawns, rugs, furniture, and so forth.
✔ Attack fleas with professionals. Your veterinarian is one but so is your exterminator. Get help for the pet from the animal practitioner. Get help for the house and yard from the exterminator.
✔ Be aware that everywhere that your Giant has been has fleas if your dog does. This includes vehicles other than the family car, the summer house, or the cabin at the lake. Fleas must be killed in all the locations where they could exist, or they will rapidly return to your dog and you.
✔ Always use care if you try to deal with fleas yourself. Use the right product for the right pet (ages and weights are important).

Ticks Another loathsome pest to infest your pet is the tick. Because ticks are much larger than fleas (and much slower), they can be spotted more easily as they siphon off some of your Giant's blood. Ticks engorge themselves and double and then triple their size all at the expense of your pet. After filling themselves, ticks (the females are the large ones and the males are the little hangers-on) drop off your pet. The females then lay their eggs (each female tick can lay thousands of eggs). The hatchling ticks or seed ticks find bushes and grass to cling to until a dog, human, or some wild animal passes by for them to hitch a ride on.

Don't put unnecessary health hurdles in your Giant's way by failing to schedule regular veterinary visits.

Ticks are not only ugly and bad for your pet, they also carry some quite serious diseases. The most notorious tick-borne disease is *Borrelia burgdorferi*, or what is commonly called Lyme disease. It is carried by deer ticks. This illness can, if left untreated, be serious or even fatal. While most states in the United States have reported incidents of Lyme disease, the main areas of infestation seem to be New England and the surrounding states, the northern Midwest states, and the West Coast states.

Quick Health Reference Chart

Concerns for All Breeds

Accidents
Heatstrokes
Bleeding

Concerns Especially for Giants

Canine hip dysplasia
Hypothyroidism
Epilepsy
Cancer
Gastric torsion (bloat)

Lyme disease (named after Lyme, Connecticut, where the first case of the illness was found) is treatable. Preventives for dogs have been introduced and may soon help eliminate this problem from dogs and people who own dogs.

Other parasites: Mange mites and ear mites round out the parasite mob. There are two kinds of mange. Both of these are caused by mites.

Demodectic (or red) mange can be a real problem for both very old and very young dogs. Characterized by ragged, patchy spots, especially around the head, demodectic mange is the most common form of this itchy and unsightly condition.

Sarcoptic mange is also caused by a mite (which can be transmitted to humans), which burrows into the skin. Sarcoptic mange is recognized by large bare areas on a dog that are generally scratched raw by the tormented canine.

As with attempting to treat internal parasites, leave mange to the medical care professionals. Many mange miracle cures have arisen over the years, and most of them did nothing at all or worsened the dog's already sad situation. Let veterinarians manage the mange.

Ear mites are troublesome to many dogs. They live in the ear or ear canal and give their locations away by the dirty, waxy, dark residue they leave in the ear. Dogs with ear mites experience a great deal of discomfort. Violent head shaking and ear pawing can mean that ear mites have infested a pet. As with most other parasites, ear mites are best treated at an animal clinic and not at home.

Other Medical Concerns

A variety of health problems can affect all breeds of dogs. However, although the Giant is usually an extremely healthy breed, the presence of certain medical conditions should be something an informed person seeking a Giant Schnauzer should know about.

Accidents: Large, active dogs often seem to find a way to be injured at certain times in their lives. The prevention section of this chapter discussed eliminating hurtful situations. No matter how conscientious you may be, you will probably never prevent all accidents. Therefore, you need some guidelines on how to handle mishaps.

✔ Do not make things worse. Careless, hurried, or inept approaches only result in aggravating the existing injury, causing another injury, or a human being bitten by a dog in pain.

✔ Muzzle and immobilize all injured pets. Even your trusted Giant Schnauzer could bite you if it feels frightened, hurt, and confused. If you are bitten, then you have also delayed the pet from receiving the treatment it needs.

✔ Slow down when moving a nonmoving pet. Rough treatment can make a major injury out of a minor injury and a fatal injury out of a major one. Study what course of action may be best, plan that course of action, and then move deliberately at accomplishing that course of action.

✔ Giant Schnauzers are often dog-aggressive and could get into a fight. As you try to extricate your pet from a fight, do not get bitten by your dog's opponent. Take great care in stopping the fight and in seeking treatment for any injuries.

A good first aid kit for dogs is a good investment. In fact, a better investment is to have such a kit with you and at every place where you and your Giant spend time.

Heatstroke: While some injuries and accidents are unforeseeable, heatstroke is not one of these. Most heatstrokes happen because a dog's owner is being stupid. Many heatstrokes occur within the stifling confines of the family car on a warm-to-hot day. Regardless of what you read or hear anywhere else, do not leave a pet in a car when the temperature is 60°F (15.6°C) or above on a sunny (or even partly cloudy) day. To do so is to expose your pet to a horrible death in a car turned solar oven.

Speed is important now if you are to save your Giant's life. Act immediately by cooling your dog's body (a mixture of cool water and rubbing alcohol works well). Drive (sanely) to the *first* veterinary clinic you can find.

Bleeding: Your first goal when you confront a bleeding pet is to find the source of the blood. If external, and you are certain that you have the right spot, apply firm, but gentle, pressure to the wound. If the wound is on a leg or the tail, place a tourniquet between the injury and the dog's heart. Loosen the tourniquet for 30 to 60 seconds every 15 minutes. If you cannot stop the bleeding and blood loss becomes significant, transport to your veterinarian or to the nearest veterinary emergency clinic. Also take the pet to the veterinarian if the wound is quite large and gaping open.

After your pet is safely under medical care, if you do not know what caused the wound, find out. An unnoticed broken piece of glass, a jagged piece of metal, or a protruding nail may have caused the injury and could do so again.

Canine Hip Dysplasia (CHD) is a potential crippling ailment of huge proportions among many breeds of purebred dogs. It is controversial in that it may be hereditary, but it can also appear in families or lines within breeds that have had few or no occurrences of this condition before. Even dogs of mixed heritage have been diagnosed as being dysplastic.

By definition, CHD is a medical condition in which the hip socket does not fit well with the knob or head of the femur. This malformation leaves an unstable hip joint. Instead of a strong fit like a cup for the head of the femur, the CHD-affected hip socket is often quite shallow. CHD produces an unsteady, very painful, and wobbling gait.

TIP

Clinical Signs of Heatstroke

1. A dazed expression on your pet's face
2. Rapid, shallow breathing with a high fever
3. Bright red gums

The presence of CHD cannot even be determined with any degree of clinical certainty until a dog is about two years of age. The Orthopedic Foundation for Animals (OFA) has determined a widely used X-ray test for diagnosing CHD and the degree to which the malady exists within a particular dog.

Some veterinarians utilize another CHD screening test—the Penn hip test to screen for CHD in younger dogs. Both OFA testing and the Penn-hip are good information for a prospective Giant Schnauzer owner to request. Even though there is no absolute clarity about the genetic heritage of CHD, responsible breeders do not breed adult dogs that do not have good hip ratings as certified by the OFA.

Hypothyroidism: This autoimmune disease is associated with decreased thyroid function and can be very bad for a Giant Schnauzer. Enough Giants have this illness that a person seeking a young puppy of this breed should ask any breeders about how their line or family of dogs stacks up in numbers of dogs with this problem.

Large-chested dogs like the Giant are prone to gastric torsion or bloat, a dread killer in many breeds.

Dogs with hypothyroidism have a decreased metabolic rate (a terrible thing for an active dog like the Giant Schnauzer). Cold temperatures adversely affect a dog with this malady. Affected dogs become listless and do not want to do their usual activities, things they once loved to do. The dog's entire system is like it is in slow shutdown.

Epilepsy: Another medical condition that sometimes besets Giant Schnauzers is the brain disorder epilepsy. How a dog gets epilepsy has not been clearly determined, but some breeds do experience it more than others.

Young dogs, even Giant Schnauzers, gradually become adults and then seniors, and need special care at each stage of life.

Every Giant Schnauzer owner should be aware of health problems associated with the breed, be able to spot symptoms, and take the necessary action to help their dogs.

Head injuries could be a reason behind some occurrences of epilepsy and the resultant seizures. Some researchers have suggested that inadequate supplies of oxygen to unborn pups may be a cause of epilepsy. Brain tumors or abnormalities may even play a part in the onset of epilepsy.

Epilepsy is usually seen in adult dogs. It expresses itself in two different types of epilepsy-related seizures:

1. The grand mal seizure is the most severe, lasting over a minute or even a minute and a half. The affected animal has major convulsions. Its teeth are tightly clenched together. It loses consciousness and thrashes around violently. Generally, the dog voids its bowels and bladder during a grand mal seizure and may salivate profusely, even though its jaws are held tightly shut.

The petit mal seizure is much less severe. A dog with a petit mal epileptic episode might look momentarily disoriented or drugged. Most such dogs never lose consciousness.

Any dog that goes into seizures or convulsions should receive professional attention from a licensed veterinarian. However, there is a bright lining to the seemingly dark cloud of canine epilepsy. With modern oral medications, even Giant Schnauzers that suffer from grand mal form seizures can have this condition controlled and live healthy and useful lives.

From a frisky puppy to an impressive adult to a venerable senior, your Giant Schnauzer will need your love, attention, and care in each and every part of its life.

Cancer: One medical condition that concerns Giant Schnauzer breeders and breeders of most other kinds of dogs is the increasing level of cancer. While Giants are not necessarily at higher risk for cancer than any other breed, concern about cancer is understandable. This is especially appropriate when national statistics for all dogs over ten years of age suggest that a number approaching 50 percent of these older dogs died of some kind of cancer.

Cancer is a widespread disease with many variations. It can take many forms, can range from mild to particularly virulent, and can be treated with varying degrees of clinical success. Some cancers are readily observable. Other cancers remain covert and hidden.

Veterinary medical science has made great inroads into treating canine cancer. As with human cancers, surgery for removal of tumors and cancerous tissue may be an option. So too is chemotherapy and radiation therapy. In some dogs, all three of these treatment modalities have been used to add years to a dog's life.

Gastric torsion (bloat): Joining the Giant Schnauzer as possible victims of gastric torsion (commonly referred to as bloat and also known as gastric dilation volvulus) are all large dogs

TIP

Steps to Preventing Bloat

✔ Stop any physical activity or exercise after a meal.

✔ Feed several times each day rather than in one large meal.

✔ Stop excessive air intake by feeding your Giant from a raised food bowl.

✔ Give the dog water throughout the day, and do not allow excessive water drinking after a meal.

with deep chests. Giants certainly fit that description, but then so do all the true giant breeds. This condition is one of the worst ailments to strike a dog. A healthy and happy Giant can be ready for any activity and only a few hours later be near an extremely painful death. While there may be some genetic predisposition to bloat, many theories exist of the cause of this often-fatal condition.

Many experts point to an unwise combination of regular activities that, when in the right sequence, can spell disaster. The following combination may cause bloat. A large, deep-chested dog like a Giant Schnauzer partakes of

1. a single, heavy meal, followed by
2. a large amount of water, followed by
3. Heavy exercise.

Even something easy to fix has been linked to gastric torsion—feeding a large dog dry dog food on the floor or ground and then allowing heavy exercise. Several hours after a large meal, an affected large dog starts to have gastric torsion. The dog tries repeatedly and without success to vomit. The dog begins to salivate a lot and is unsteady on its feet. The abdomen becomes tightly distended. The dog's stomach has flipped over, sealing in all the food, water, stomach gases, and air into a now-closed digestive system. Without immediate help, death is certain. The dog must be rushed to a veterinary surgeon who must operate within minutes or the toxic condition of the dog will close the window on saving the pet.

Old Age

For a large dog, the Giant has a relatively long life span. One day your Giant will begin to slow a step or two. Your activities with this mature dog must gradually slow down to allow the pet not to overtax itself with the things it did years before. Just as the dog's regular diet makes way for food for older dogs, so must many aspects of the dog's life gradually adjust to the somewhat diminished energy and vigor of the aging dog.

Your family has lived up to its commitment to the Giant as a puppy and as an adult. Now another type of commitment must be made. Busy lifestyles must still make room and time for the gracefully aging dog. Do not leave the oldster out of the loop of your lives. This would be too painful for a dog that spent its youth looking after you and your household.

Knowing When to Say Good-bye

Few things in this world are sadder than having to say good-bye to a true and trusted companion whose only fault was that it loved you with all its heart. Such a brave and powerful dog deserves to die in combat against a dozen enemies, not wheezing its life away in a sunny spot on the carpet. However, valiant deaths do not always come to valiant companions.

Because you and your family have faithfully taken your pet to the veterinarian for checkups and when such visits were necessary, your veterinarian knows your veteran dog very well. Listen to your veterinarian and to your own good judgment about when enough suffering is enough. Love your old Giant Schnauzer enough to do the right thing when the time comes. Love the dog that loved you enough to die for you by loving it enough to say good-bye.

INFORMATION

Kennel Clubs
(Breed club officers normally change on a regular basis. For the most current information regarding breed club personnel, contact the national kennel club for the country you are interested in.)

American Kennel Club
5580 Centerview Drive
Suite 200
Raleigh, NC 27606
Phone: (919) 233-9767
Fax: (919) 233-3740
E-mail: *info@akc.org*
Web site: *www.akc.org*

Canadian Kennel Club
89 Skyway Avenue
Suite 100
Etobicoke, Ontario M9W 6R4
Canada
Phone: (416) 675-6506

The Kennel Club (England)
1-4 Clarges Street
Picadilly
London W7Y 8AB
England

Australian National Kennel Council
Royal Show Grounds
Ascot Vale
Victoria,
Australia

New Zealand Kennel Club
P.O. Box 523
Wellington 1
New Zealand

Giant Schnauzer Organizations
Giant Schnauzer Club of America, Inc.
Secretary—Kathy DeShong
7855 Whistling Winds Lane
Brighton, IL 62012
E-mail: GSCAMERICA@aol.com
(618)466-6768

Giant Schnauzer Club of Canada
Linda Robb, Secretary
RR 3 Box 227
Durham, Ontario N0G 1R0
Canada
Web site: *http://www.schnauzerware.net/GSCanada/index.shtml*

Working Schnauzer Federation—America
c/o Tami Huber
P.O. Box 453
Citrus Heights, CA 95611-0453
Phone: (916) 966-6999
E-mail: tamihuber@aol.com
Web Site: *http://members.aol.com/dogs4wsf/*

Giant Schnauzer Club of America Rescue
Carolyn Janak, *National Rescue Coordinator*
1691 So Arbutus
Lakewood, CO 80228
(Home) (303) 988-6564
(Work) (303) 233-0355

Periodicals

Dog Fancy Magazine
P.O. Box 6050
Mission Viejo, CA 92690

Dog World
260 Madison Avenue
New York, NY 10016

Books

Alderton, David. *The Dog Care Manual.* Hauppauge, New York: Barron's Educational Series, Inc., 1989.

American Kennel Club. *The Complete Dog Book,* 19th Edition Revised. New York: Howell Book House, 1997.

Baer, Ted. *Communicating with Your Dog.* Hauppauge, New York: Barron's Educational Series, Inc., 1989.

Bailey, Gwen. *The Well-Behaved Dog.* Hauppauge, New York: Barron's Educational Series, Inc., 1998.

Coile, D. Caroline. *Show Me! A Dog Show Primer.* Hauppauge, New York: Barron's Educational Series, Inc., 1997.

Klever, Ulrich. *The Complete Book of Dog Care.* Hauppauge, New York: Barron's Educational Series, Inc., 1989.

Rice, Dan. *The Dog Handbook.* Hauppauge, New York: Barron's Educational Series, Inc., 1999.

Smith, Cheryl S., and Stephanie J. Tauton. *The Trick Is in the Training.* Hauppauge, New York: Barron's Educational Series, Inc., 1998.

Streitferdt, Uwe. *Healthy Dog, Happy Dog.* Hauppauge, New York: Barron's Educational Series, Inc., 1994.

Walker, Joan Hustace. *The Rottweiler Handbook.* Hauppauge, New York: Barron's Educational Series, Inc., 2001.

INDEX

About the Author

Joe Stahlkuppe is a widely read pet columnist, author, and freelance feature writer. A long-time fan of purebred dogs and a member of the Dog Writers Association of America, he has written several Barron's Pet Owner's Manuals and dog breed Handbooks. A consultant to the pet industry, Joe divides his free time between his grandchildren, Catie, Peter Joel, and Julia, and his role as an ordained clergyman/pastor of a small church in Brookside, Alabama.

Photo Credits

Pets by Paulette: pages 3, 4, 5, 8 top, 8 bottom right, 9 top, 9 bottom right, 13, 16, 17, 20 bottom left, 21 top right, 24 top right, 36, 37, 40 top, 44, 53, 61 right, 65, 72, 73, 76, 77, 89 right, 92, 93; Kent and Donna Dannen: pages 8 bottom left, 9 bottom left, 12, 20 top right, 21 bottom, 25 bottom left, 29, 33, 40 bottom, 45, 49 bottom, 60 left, 64, 68; Curtis Hustace: pages 20 top left, 20 bottom right, 21 top left, 24 top left, 24 bottom left, 24 bottom right, 25 top left, 25 top right, 25 bottom right, 41, 49 top, 52, 56, 57, 60 right, 61 left, 69, 80, 81, 84, 85, 88, 89 left.

Cover Photos

Front cover and inside front cover: Donna Coss; Back cover and inside back cover: Tara Darling

Important Note

This book is concerned with selecting, keeping, and raising Giant Schnauzers. The publisher and the author think it is important to point out that the advice and information for Giant Schnauzer maintenance applies to healthy, normally developed animals. Anyone who acquires an adult dog or one from an animal shelter must consider that the animal may have behavioral problems and may, for example, bite without any visible provocation. Such anxiety biters are dangerous for the owner as well as the general public.

Caution is further advised in the association of children with dogs, in meetings with other dogs, and in exercising the dog without a leash.

All inquiries should be addressed to:
Barron's Educational Series, Inc.
250 Wireless Boulevard
Hauppauge, NY 11788
http://www.barronseduc.com

International Standard Book No. 0-7641-1884-6

Library of Congress Catalog Card No. 2001037940

Library of Congress Cataloging-in-Publication Data
Stahlkuppe, Joe..
Giant Schnauzers : everything about purchase, care, nutrition, training, and wellness / Joe Stahlkuppe.
p. cm. — (A complete pet owner's manual)
Includes bibliographical references (p.).
ISBN 0-7641-1884-6 (alk. paper)
1. Giant schnauzer. I. Title. II. Series.
SF429.G5 S73 2002
636.73—dc21 2001037940

Printed in Hong Kong

9 8 7 6 5 4 3 2 1